Recipes from Grandma's Kitchen™

Grandma's Favorites

pil

Publications International, Ltd.

Favorite Brand Name Recipes at www.fbnr.com

Interior illustrations by Jan Gregg-Kelm.

Cover illustration by Judy Blankenship.

ISBN: 1-4127-2043-5

Library of Congress Control Number: 2004110630

Manufactured in China.

8 7 6 5 4 3 2 1

Microwave Cooking: Microwave ovens vary in wattage. Use the cooking times as guidelines and check for doneness before adding more time.

Preparation/Cooking Times: Preparation times are based on the approximate amount of time required to assemble the recipe before cooking, baking, chilling or serving. These times include preparation steps such as measuring, chopping and mixing. The fact that some preparations and cooking can be done simultaneously is taken into account. Preparation of optional ingredients and serving suggestions is not included.

Table of Contents

Fresh-Baked Breads

Apple Pecan Muffins

½ cup water
1 egg, lightly beaten
¼ cup frozen apple juice concentrate, thawed, undiluted
2 tablespoons butter, melted
2 cups buttermilk baking mix
½ cup chopped pecans
¼ cup sugar
¼ teaspoon ground cinnamon

1. Preheat oven to 400°F. Grease or paper-line 12 regular size (2½-inch) muffin cups.

2. Fit processor with steel blade. Place water, egg, apple juice and butter into work bowl. Process using on/off pulsing action 3 or 4 times to mix.

3. Add baking mix, pecans, sugar and cinnamon; process using on/off pulsing action just until flour is moistened. *Do not overprocess.* Batter should be lumpy.

4. Spoon batter into muffin cups, filling each about ⅔ full. Bake 12 to 15 minutes until golden or until toothpick inserted in centers comes out clean. Cool in pan or on wire rack 5 minutes. Remove from pan; serve warm.   *Makes 1 dozen muffins*

Streusel-Topped Cinnamon Chips Muffins

    1 egg
    ¾ cup milk
    ⅓ cup vegetable oil
 1¾ cups all-purpose flour
    ⅓ cup sugar
    1 tablespoon baking powder
    ½ teaspoon salt
 1⅔ cups (10 ounce package) HERSHEY₊S Cinnamon Chips
    Streusel Topping (recipe follows)

1. Heat oven to 400°F. Line muffin cups (2½ inches in diameter) with paper bake cups.

2. Beat egg in bowl. Stir in milk and oil. Combine flour, sugar, baking powder and salt; add to egg mixture, stirring just until dry ingredients are moistened. Gently stir in chips. Fill muffin cups ⅔ full with batter. Sprinkle Streusel Topping over top.

3. Bake 20 minutes or until golden. Cool in cups 5 minutes; remove. Serve warm.

Makes 12 to 14 muffins

Streusel Topping: Combine ¼ cup all-purpose flour, 2 tablespoons sugar and 2 tablespoons softened butter or margarine; mix with fork until crumbly.

Zucchini Nut Bread

2 eggs
½ cup vegetable oil
1½ cups all-purpose flour
1 cup chopped nuts or ½ cup each raisins and nuts
1 cup shredded zucchini
¾ cup sugar
1½ teaspoons ground cinnamon
1 teaspoon baking soda
1 teaspoon vanilla
½ teaspoon salt
½ teaspoon baking powder

1. Preheat oven to 375°F. Grease 8½×4½-inch loaf pan or two 5¾×3¼-inch loaf pans.

2. Fit processor with steel blade. Measure all ingredients into work bowl. Process just until flour is moistened, 5 to 10 seconds. Do not overprocess. Batter should be lumpy.

3. Pour batter into prepared pan. Bake 1 hour for larger loaf or 30 to 35 minutes for smaller loaves or until toothpick inserted into center comes out clean. Cool bread 15 minutes in pan. Transfer to wire rack; cool completely.

Makes 1 large or 2 small loaves

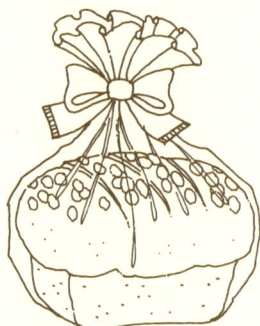

Banana Chocolate Chip Muffins

2 ripe, medium DOLE® Bananas
1 cup packed brown sugar
2 eggs
½ cup margarine, melted
1 teaspoon vanilla extract
2¼ cups all-purpose flour
2 teaspoons baking powder
½ teaspoon ground cinnamon
½ teaspoon salt
1 cup chocolate chips
½ cup chopped walnuts

• Purée bananas in blender (1 cup). Beat bananas, sugar, eggs, margarine and vanilla in medium bowl until well blended.

• Combine flour, baking powder, cinnamon and salt in large bowl. Stir in chocolate chips and nuts. Make well in center of dry ingredients. Add banana mixture. Stir just until blended. Spoon into well greased 2½-inch muffin pan cups.

• Bake at 350°F 25 to 30 minutes or until toothpick inserted in centers comes out clean. Cool slightly; remove from pan and place on wire rack.

Makes 12 muffins

Prep Time: 20 minutes
Bake Time: 30 minutes

Egg Twists

6 to 6½ cups all-purpose flour
2 packages RED STAR® Active Dry Yeast or QUICK•RISE™ Yeast
3 tablespoons sugar
1 tablespoon salt
1 cup milk
½ cup water
¼ cup butter
4 eggs, lightly beaten (reserve 1 tablespoon)
1 tablespoon water
Sesame seeds

In large mixer bowl, combine 3 cups flour, yeast, sugar and salt; mix well. Heat milk, ½ cup water and butter until very warm (120°-130°F); butter does not need to melt). Add to flour mixture. Add eggs. Blend at low speed until moistened; beat 3 minutes at medium speed. By hand, gradually stir in enough remaining flour to make a firm dough. Knead on floured surface until smooth and elastic, 5 to 8 minutes. Place in greased bowl, turning to grease top. Cover; let rise in warm place about 1 hour (40 minutes for Quick•Rise™ Yeast).

Punch down dough. On lightly floured surface, roll dough to 12-inch square. Cut into four 3-inch-wide strips. Twist 2 strips together; repeat with remaining strips. Place in greased 9×5-inch bread pans. Cover; let rise in warm place about 40 minutes (30 minutes for Quick•Rise™ Yeast). Preheat oven to 375°F. Combine reserved egg and 1 tablespoon water. Brush on loaves. Sprinkle with sesame seeds. Bake at 375°F for 35 to 40 minutes until golden brown. Remove from pans; cool.

Makes 2 loaves

Oatmeal Walnut Bread or Pan Rolls

2⅔ to 3 cups all-purpose flour
4½ teaspoons (2 packets) RED STAR® QUICK•RISE™ Yeast
    or Bread Machine Yeast or Active Dry Yeast
2 teaspoons salt
1½ cups water
⅓ cup molasses
4 teaspoons vegetable oil
⅔ cup rolled oats
1⅓ cups whole wheat flour
1 cup chopped walnuts
1 egg, slightly beaten
1 tablespoon water
2 tablespoons rolled oats

In large mixer bowl, combine 2 cups all-purpose flour, yeast, and salt; mix well. In saucepan, heat 1½ cups water, molasses, vegetable oil, and rolled oats until very warm (120 to 130°F). Add to flour mixture. Blend at low speed until moistened; beat 3 minutes at medium speed. By hand, gradually stir in whole wheat flour, nuts, and enough remaining all-purpose flour to make a firm dough. Knead on floured surface 5 to 8 minutes. (Dough will be slightly sticky.) Place in greased bowl, turning to grease top. Cover; let rise in warm place about 30 minutes (45 minutes for Active Dry Yeast).

Punch down dough. Divide into 2 parts. Shape each part into round loaf or pan rolls. Place round loaves on greased baking sheet or pan rolls in two 8-inch square greased pans. Cover; let rise in warm place about 30 minutes (45 minutes for Active Dry Yeast). Combine egg and 1 tablespoon water; brush tops. Sprinkle with rolled oats. Bake in preheated oven at 375°F for 30 to 40 minutes. Remove from pan; cool.

Makes 2 round loaves (18 to 24 rolls)

Plan Ahead:
Parbake bread or rolls at 400°F for 15 minutes. Remove from pan; cool. Wrap tightly and freeze for later use. To serve, thaw, then bake at 425°F for 7 minutes.

Super Cinnamon Bun

Cinnamon Bun

   1 package (16 ounces) hot roll mix
   1 cup QUAKER® Oats (quick or old fashioned, uncooked)
   ¾ cup raisins
   ½ cup granulated sugar, divided
 2½ teaspoons ground cinnamon, divided
   1 cup hot water (120°F to 130°F)
   1 egg, lightly beaten
   5 tablespoons margarine or butter, melted, divided

Glaze

   ¾ cup powdered sugar
   3 to 4 teaspoons milk
   ½ teaspoon vanilla

Lightly grease large cookie sheet. In large bowl, combine hot roll mix, yeast packet, oats, raisins, ¼ cup sugar and 1½ teaspoons cinnamon. Stir in hot water, egg and 3 tablespoons melted margarine. Mix until dough pulls away from sides of bowl. Knead on lightly floured surface 5 minutes or until smooth and elastic. Divide into 4 equal pieces; roll each piece into 12-inch rope on lightly floured surface. In center of prepared cookie sheet, form a coil with one rope. Attach a second rope to the coiled rope by pressing the rope ends together firmly; continue coiling around the first rope. Repeat with the third and fourth ropes to form one large bun.

Combine remaining ¼ cup sugar, 1 teaspoon cinnamon and 2 tablespoons melted margarine. Brush evenly over top and sides of bun. Cover loosely with plastic wrap; let rise in warm place 30 minutes or until about double in size.

Heat oven to 375°F. Bake 30 to 35 minutes or until golden brown. Carefully remove to wire rack; cool slightly. For glaze, combine all ingredients; mix until smooth. Drizzle over bun. Serve warm or at room temperature.

Makes 16 servings

Note: If hot roll mix is not available, combine 3 cups all-purpose flour, 1 cup oats, ¾ cup raisins, two ¼-ounce packages quick-rising yeast, ⅓ cup granulated sugar, 1½ teaspoons salt and 1½ teaspoons cinnamon. Continue as recipe directs.

Fresh-Baked Breads

Hot Cross Buns

1 package (¼ ounce) active dry yeast
¼ cup warm water (105° to 115°F)
¾ cup warm milk
¼ cup GRANDMA'S® Molasses
2 eggs
4 tablespoons (½ stick) butter, softened
1½ teaspoons salt
3½ cups all-purpose flour, divided
1 teaspoon cinnamon
½ teaspoon nutmeg
¼ teaspoon allspice
½ cup currants or raisins
2 tablespoons chopped candied citron

1. In large bowl, stir yeast into water and let stand several minutes to dissolve. Combine milk, molasses, eggs, butter and salt in large bowl; beat well. Add yeast mixture; mix well. Beat in 1½ cups flour, cinnamon, nutmeg and allspice. Cover bowl and let rise about 1 hour or until bubbly or double in bulk.

2. Add remaining 2 cups flour and blend well, adding additional flour if necessary to make dough firm enough to handle. Turn onto floured surface; knead dough until firm and elastic. Add currants and citron during last 5 minutes of kneading. Place dough in greased bowl; cover and let rise until double in bulk.

3. Heat oven to 375°F. Punch dough down; turn onto lightly floured surface. Roll into 14×10-inch rectangle, about ½ inch thick. Cut dough with 2½- to 3-inch round cutter; place buns about 1 inch apart on greased baking sheets. Gather up scraps, reroll and continue cutting until all dough has been used. Let rise, uncovered, until double in bulk.

4. Just before baking, use floured scissors to snip cross in top of each bun, cutting about ½ inch deep. Bake about 15 minutes or until tops of buns are golden brown. Remove from oven and transfer to rack to cool. *Makes 12 buns*

Lemon Blueberry Loaf

Bread
1 package DUNCAN HINES® Bakery-Style Wild Maine Blueberry Muffin Mix
½ cup dairy sour cream
½ cup milk
1 egg
1 tablespoon grated lemon peel (see Tip)
½ cup chopped pecans

Glaze
⅓ cup granulated sugar
2 tablespoons lemon juice

1. Preheat oven to 350°F. Grease and flour 9×5-inch loaf pan.

2. Rinse blueberries from Mix with cold water and drain.

3. For bread, empty muffin mix into medium bowl. Break up any lumps. Add sour cream, milk, egg and grated lemon peel. Stir until moistened, about 50 strokes. Fold in blueberries and pecans. Pour into pan. Bake at 350°F 60 to 65 minutes or until toothpick inserted in center comes out clean. Poke holes in top of warm loaf with toothpick or long-tined fork.

4. For glaze, combine sugar and lemon juice in small saucepan. Cook on medium heat, stirring constantly, until sugar dissolves. Spoon hot glaze evenly over loaf. Cool in pan 15 minutes. Loosen loaf from pan. Invert onto cooling rack. Turn right side up. Cool completely.   *Makes 1 loaf (12 slices)*

Tip: When grating lemon peel, avoid the bitter white portion known as the pith.

Cherry Nut Coffee Cake

Topping
- ⅓ cup granulated sugar
- ¼ cup all-purpose flour
- ¼ Butter Flavor CRISCO® Stick or ¼ cup Butter Flavor CRISCO® Shortening
- ½ cup sliced almonds or other chopped nuts

Cake
- ¾ Butter Flavor CRISCO® Stick or ¾ cup Butter Flavor CRISCO® Shortening
- 1¼ cups granulated sugar
- 1 teaspoon vanilla
- 3 medium eggs
- 3 cups all-purpose flour
- 1½ teaspoons baking soda
- 1 teaspoon salt
- 1½ cups sour cream
- 1 can (21 ounces) cherry pie filling

Glaze
- Milk
- 1 cup confectioners' sugar
- ½ teaspoon almond extract

Preheat oven to 350°F. Spray 13×9-inch pan with CRISCO® No-Stick Cooking Spray.

For Topping, combine sugar and flour in small bowl. Mix in CRISCO® Shortening until crumbly.

For Cake, beat together CRISCO® Shortening, sugar and vanilla in large bowl. Add eggs, beating well. Combine flour, baking soda and salt in medium bowl. Add to CRISCO® mixture alternately with sour cream. Spread half the batter in greased pan. Cover with half the cherry pie filling, spreading as evenly as possible. Repeat layers. Sprinkle with almonds and topping mixture. Bake for 50 minutes or until top is brown and wooden pick inserted in center comes out clean. Cool until slightly warm or to room temperature.

For Glaze, add enough milk (about 1 tablespoon) to confectioners' sugar to make desired consistency. Stir in almond extract. Drizzle over cake.

Makes 1 (13×9-inch) coffee cake

Peanut Butter and Jelly Muffins

PAM® No-Stick Cooking Spray
2½ cups all-purpose flour
¾ cup sugar
1½ tablespoons baking powder
1 teaspoon salt
⅔ cup PETER PAN® Extra Crunchy Peanut Butter
¾ cup milk
⅓ cup WESSON® Vegetable Oil
2 eggs, room temperature and beaten
1 jar (10 ounces) KNOTT'S BERRY FARM® Jelly or Preserves, any flavor

Preheat oven to 400°F. Spray 12 muffin cups with PAM Cooking Spray. In a large mixing bowl, stir together flour, sugar, baking powder and salt. Using a pastry cutter or two knives, cut Peter Pan Peanut Butter into flour until mixture resembles coarse crumbs. Add milk, Wesson Oil and eggs; stir until just moistened. Spoon muffin cups *½ full* with batter, creating a well in the center of each cup. Place a heaping *1 tablespoon* of Knott's Jelly into well. Evenly distribute remaining batter over jelly. Bake 20 to 25 minutes or until wooden pick inserted into center comes out clean. Cool completely on wire rack. *Makes 1 dozen muffins*

Prep Time: 15 minutes
Bake Time: 25 minutes

Savory Cheese Bread

6 to 7 cups all-purpose flour, divided
2 tablespoons sugar
4 teaspoons instant minced onion
2 teaspoons salt
2 packages active dry yeast
½ teaspoon caraway seeds
1¾ cups milk
½ cup water
3 tablespoons butter or margarine
1 teaspoon TABASCO® brand Pepper Sauce
2 cups (8 ounces) shredded sharp Cheddar cheese, divided
1 egg, lightly beaten

Combine 2½ cups flour, sugar, onion, salt, yeast and caraway seeds in large bowl of electric mixer. Combine milk, water and butter in small saucepan. Heat milk mixture until very warm (120° to 130°F); stir in TABASCO® Sauce.

With mixer at medium speed, gradually add milk mixture to dry ingredients; beat 2 minutes. Add 1 cup flour. Beat at high speed 2 minutes. With wooden spoon stir in 1½ cups cheese and enough flour to make a stiff dough. Turn dough out onto lightly floured surface. Knead 8 to 10 minutes or until dough is smooth and elastic, adding as much remaining flour as needed to prevent sticking. Place dough in large greased bowl and turn once to grease surface. Cover with towel; let rise in warm place (90° to 100°F) 1 hour or until doubled in bulk.

Punch dough down. Divide dough into 16 equal pieces; shape each piece into a ball. Place half the balls in well-greased 10-inch tube pan. Sprinkle with remaining ½ cup cheese. Arrange remaining balls on top. Cover with towel; let rise in warm place 45 minutes or until doubled in bulk. Preheat oven to 375°F. Brush dough with egg. Bake 40 to 50 minutes or until golden brown. Remove from pan. Cool completely on wire rack.

Makes 1 (10-inch) round loaf

Banana Blueberry Muffins

2 ripe, medium DOLE® Bananas
6 tablespoons margarine
6 tablespoons brown sugar
1 egg
1½ cups all-purpose flour
½ teaspoon baking powder
½ teaspoon baking soda
½ teaspoon salt
½ teaspoon grated lemon peel
1 cup frozen blueberries, rinsed, drained

• Purée bananas in blender (1 cup).

• Beat margarine and sugar in large bowl until light and fluffy. Mix in bananas and egg.

• Combine flour, baking powder, baking soda, salt and lemon peel in medium bowl. Blend into margarine mixture just until moistened. Fold in blueberries.

• Line 6 large muffin cups with paper liners; spray lightly with vegetable cooking spray. Spoon batter evenly into cups.

• Bake at 375°F 20 to 25 minutes.   *Makes 6 muffins*

Prep Time: 20 minutes
Bake Time: 25 minutes

Irish Soda Bread

    5 cups all-purpose flour
    1 cup sugar
    1 tablespoon baking powder
1½ teaspoons salt
    1 teaspoon baking soda
½ Butter Flavor CRISCO® Stick, cut into cubes, room temperature
        or ½ cup Butter Flavor CRISCO® Shortening
2½ cups raisins
    3 tablespoons caraway seeds
2½ cups buttermilk
    1 egg

Preheat oven to 350°F.

Generously grease a heavy ovenproof 10-inch skillet. Whisk first 5 ingredients in large bowl until blended. Add CRISCO® Shortening; using fingertips, rub in until coarse crumbs form. Stir in raisins and caraway seeds.

Whisk buttermilk and egg in medium bowl until blended. Add to dough; using wooden spoon, stir just until incorporated (dough will be very sticky).

Transfer dough to prepared skillet; smooth top, mounding slightly in center. Using small sharp knife dipped in flour; cut 1-inch-deep "X" in center of dough. Bake about 1 hour 15 minutes or until tester inserted into center comes out clean.

Cool bread in skillet 10 minutes. Remove from skillet and cool completely on wire rack.

To store leftovers, wrap tightly in foil and store at room temperature.

Makes 14 to 16 servings

Variation: This bread is also great toasted and served with your favorite SMUCKER'S® Jam.

Pumpkin Bread

2 cups (15-ounce can) pumpkin
1 cup vegetable oil
4 eggs
⅔ cup water
3½ cups all-purpose flour
3 cups sugar
2 teaspoons baking soda
1½ teaspoons salt
1 teaspoon ground cinnamon
1⅔ cups (10-ounce package) REESE'S® Peanut Butter Chips
1 cup chopped nuts
1 cup raisins (optional)

1. Heat oven to 350°F. Grease and flour three 8½×4½×2½-inch loaf pans.

2. Stir together pumpkin, oil, eggs and water in large bowl. Stir together flour, sugar, baking soda, salt and cinnamon; gradually add to pumpkin mixture, stirring until well blended. Stir in peanut butter chips, nuts and raisins, if desired. Pour evenly into prepared pans.

3. Bake 55 to 65 minutes or until wooden pick inserted in center comes out clean. Cool 10 minutes; remove from pans to wire racks. Cool completely.

Makes 3 loaves (36 servings)

Peanut Butter Chip & Banana Mini Muffins

    2 cups all-purpose biscuit baking mix
    ¼ cup sugar
    2 tablespoons butter or margarine, softened
    1 egg
    1 cup mashed very ripe bananas (2 to 3 medium)
    1 cup REESE'S® Peanut Butter Chips
      Quick Glaze (recipe follows, optional)

1. Heat oven to 400°F. Grease small muffin cups (1¾ inches in diameter).

2. Stir together baking mix, sugar, butter and egg in medium bowl; with fork, beat vigorously for 30 seconds. Stir in bananas and peanut butter chips. Fill muffin cups ⅔ full with batter.

3. Bake 12 to 15 minutes or until golden brown. Meanwhile, prepare Quick Glaze, if desired. Immediately remove muffins from pan; dip tops of warm muffins into glaze. Serve warm.   *Makes about 4 dozen small muffins*

Quick Glaze

    1½ cups powdered sugar
    2 tablespoons water

Stir together powdered sugar and water in small bowl until smooth and of desired consistency. Add additional water, ½ teaspoon at a time, if needed.

Banana-Nana Pecan Bread

1 cup QUAKER® Oats (quick or old fashioned, uncooked)
½ cup chopped pecans
3 tablespoons margarine or butter, melted
2 tablespoons firmly packed brown sugar
1 (14-ounce) package banana bread quick bread mix
1 cup water
½ cup mashed ripe banana
2 eggs, lightly beaten
3 tablespoons vegetable oil

Heat oven to 375°F. Grease and flour bottom only of 9×5-inch loaf pan. Combine oats, pecans, margarine and sugar; mix well. Reserve ½ cup oat mixture for topping; set aside. In bowl, combine remaining oat mixture, quick bread mix, water, banana, eggs and oil. Mix just until dry ingredients are moistened. Pour into prepared pan. Sprinkle top of loaf with reserved oat mixture. Bake 50 to 55 minutes or until wooden pick inserted in center comes out clean. Cool 10 minutes in pan; remove to wire rack. Cool.   *Makes 12 servings*

Blueberry Sour Cream Tea Ring

Streusel
- ¼ cup firmly packed brown sugar
- ¼ cup chopped pecans
- ½ teaspoon ground cinnamon

Cake
- 1 package DUNCAN HINES® Bakery-Style Wild Maine Blueberry Muffin Mix
- ¾ cup dairy sour cream
- 1 egg
- 2 tablespoons water

Glaze
- ½ cup confectioners' sugar
- 1 tablespoon milk

1. Preheat oven to 350°F. Grease 7-cup tube pan.

2. For streusel, combine brown sugar, pecans and cinnamon in small bowl. Set aside.

3. Rinse blueberries from Mix with cold water and drain.

4. For cake, empty muffin mix into bowl. Break up any lumps. Add sour cream, egg and water. Stir until blended. Pour one-third of batter into pan. Sprinkle half of streusel over batter. Place half of blueberries over streusel. Repeat layers ending with batter on top. Bake at 350°F for 33 to 37 minutes or until toothpick inserted in center comes out clean. Cool in pan 10 minutes. Invert onto cooling rack. Turn right-side-up.

5. For glaze, combine confectioners' sugar and milk in small bowl. Stir until smooth. Drizzle over warm cake. *Makes 12 servings*

Corn Bread Wedges

1 package corn bread mix
1 cup (4 ounces) finely grated sharp Cheddar cheese
¼ cup butter or margarine, softened
¼ teaspoon Worcestershire sauce
¼ teaspoon TABASCO® brand Pepper Sauce
1 egg white, stiffly beaten
Paprika

Prepare corn bread according to package directions and bake in 9-inch pie plate. Meanwhile, combine cheese, butter, Worcestershire sauce and TABASCO® Sauce; beat until smooth. Fold in egg white.

Cut corn bread into 8 wedges; spread evenly with cheese mixture. Sprinkle with paprika. Set oven to broil; broil about 4 minutes or until cheese topping melts and becomes puffy and golden brown.	*Makes 8 servings*

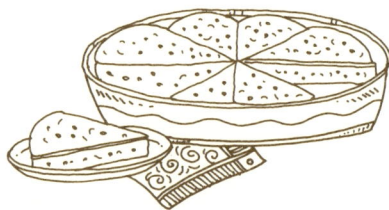

Lemon Cranberry Loaves

1¼ cups finely chopped fresh cranberries
½ cup finely chopped walnuts
¼ cup granulated sugar
1 package DUNCAN HINES® Moist Deluxe® Lemon Supreme Cake Mix
¾ cup milk
1 package (3 ounces) cream cheese, softened
4 eggs
Confectioners' sugar

1. Preheat oven to 350°F. Grease and flour two 8½×4½-inch loaf pans.

2. Stir together cranberries, walnuts and granulated sugar in large bowl; set aside.

3. Combine cake mix, milk and cream cheese in large bowl. Beat at medium speed with electric mixer for 2 minutes. Add eggs, 1 at a time, beating for 2 minutes. Fold in cranberry mixture. Pour into prepared pans. Bake at 350°F for 45 to 50 minutes or until toothpick inserted in centers comes out clean. Cool in pans 15 minutes. Loosen loaves from pans. Invert onto cooling rack. Turn right side up. Cool completely. Dust with confectioners' sugar.

Makes 2 loaves (24 servings)

Tip: To quickly chop cranberries or walnuts, use a food processor fitted with a steel blade and pulse until evenly chopped.

Country-Style Soups & Stews

Hearty Beef Barley Stew

1 tablespoon BERTOLLI® Olive Oil
1½ pounds beef stew meat
2 cups baby carrots
1 package (8 ounces) fresh mushrooms, sliced
1 envelope LIPTON® RECIPE SECRETS® Onion Soup Mix
2 cups (14½ ounces each) beef broth
1 can (14½ ounces) diced tomatoes, undrained
2 cups water
¾ cup barley
1 cup frozen peas

1. In 6-quart saucepot, heat olive oil over medium-high heat, brown beef, stirring occasionally, 4 minutes.

2. Stir in remaining ingredients except peas.

3. Bring to a boil over high heat. Reduce heat to medium-low and simmer, covered, stirring occasionally, 1½ hours or until beef is tender. Stir in peas. Cook 5 minutes or until heated through.   *Makes 6 servings*

Slow Cooker Method: In slow cooker, layer carrots, mushrooms and beef. Combine soup mix, broth, tomatoes, water and barley; pour over beef and vegetables. Cook, covered, on HIGH 4 to 6 hours or LOW 8 to 10 hours. Stir in peas and cook, covered, 5 minutes or until heated through. Season, if desired, with salt and pepper.

Prep Time: 10 minutes
Cook Time: 1 hour 40 minutes

Country-Style *Soups & Stews*

Stick-to-Your-Ribs Hearty Beef Stew

1½ pounds lean beef stew meat, cut into bite-size pieces
¼ cup all-purpose flour
½ teaspoon seasoned salt
⅓ cup WESSON® Vegetable Oil
2 medium onions, cut into 1-inch pieces
1 (14.5-ounce) can beef broth
1 (8-ounce) can HUNT'S® Tomato Sauce
4 medium potatoes, peeled and cubed
5 stalks celery, cut into 1-inch pieces
6 carrots, peeled and cut into 1-inch pieces
1½ teaspoons salt
½ teaspoon Italian seasoning
½ teaspoon pepper
1 tablespoon cornstarch plus 2 tablespoons water

In a bag, toss beef with flour and seasoned salt until well coated. In a large Dutch oven, in hot Wesson® Oil, brown beef with onions until onions are tender. Add *remaining* ingredients *except* cornstarch mixture; stir until well blended. Bring to a boil; reduce heat and simmer, covered, for 1 hour 15 minutes or until beef is tender. Stir cornstarch mixture; whisk into stew. Continue to cook an additional 10 minutes, stirring occasionally or until mixture thickens.

Makes 6 to 8 servings

Tip: For a fancier stew, reduce beef broth by ½ cup and add ½ cup red wine.

Sweet 'n' Sour Turkey Meatball Stew

2 pounds ground turkey
¾ cup dry bread crumbs
½ cup chopped onion
⅓ cup chopped water chestnuts
4 tablespoons reduced-sodium soy sauce, divided
1 clove garlic, minced
1 egg
½ teaspoon salt
½ teaspoon ground ginger
¼ teaspoon black pepper
2 tablespoons vegetable oil
2 cups water
¼ cup sugar
¼ cup apple cider vinegar
1 can (20 ounces) pineapple chunks in juice, drained and juice reserved
1 each medium green and red bell pepper, cut into ½-inch pieces
   Peel from 1 lemon, coarsely chopped
2 tablespoons cornstarch
   Hot cooked rice (optional)

1. Combine turkey, bread crumbs, onion, water chestnuts, 1 tablespoon soy sauce, garlic, egg, salt, ginger and black pepper in large bowl; mix well. Shape into meatballs.*

2. Heat oil in 5-quart Dutch oven over medium heat. Brown meatballs. Remove with slotted spoon; discard fat. Combine water, sugar, vinegar and reserved pineapple juice in Dutch oven. Return meatballs to Dutch oven. Bring to a boil over high heat. Reduce heat to low. Cover; simmer 20 to 25 minutes. Stir in pineapple, bell peppers and lemon peel. Simmer, uncovered, 5 minutes.

3. Combine remaining 3 tablespoons soy sauce and cornstarch in small bowl; blend until smooth. Bring meatballs to a boil over medium-high heat; stir in cornstarch mixture. Cook 5 minutes or until mixture thickens, stirring constantly. Serve over rice, if desired.   *Makes 6 servings*

To shape uniform meatballs, place meat mixture on a cutting board; pat evenly into a large square, 1 inch thick. With sharp knife, cut into 1-inch squares; shape into balls.

Herbed Pork and Vegetable Stew

4 boneless pork chops, cut into ¾-inch cubes
2 teaspoons olive oil
⅓ cup flour
2 (14½-ounce) cans beef broth
1 (14½-ounce) can diced tomatoes with garlic and onion
3 bay leaves
1 teaspoon dried marjoram leaves
½ teaspoon hot pepper sauce
¼ teaspoon salt
8 small new potatoes, quartered
1 (16-ounce) package baby carrots
1 (16-ounce) package small frozen pearl onions

Heat oven to 350°F. In a large nonstick skillet heat oil; cook pork, half at a time, for 2 to 3 minutes or until browned. Remove pork from skillet, reserving drippings. Transfer pork to a 4-quart casserole. Stir flour into drippings; stir in broth, tomatoes, bay leaves, marjoram, hot pepper sauce and salt. Cook and stir until thickened and bubbly. Stir tomato mixture into pork. Add potatoes, carrots and onions. Bake, covered, for 55 to 60 minutes or until carrots are crisp-tender, stirring occasionally. Remove bay leaves. To serve, ladle into soup bowls. *Makes 6 servings*

Favorite recipe from **National Pork Board**

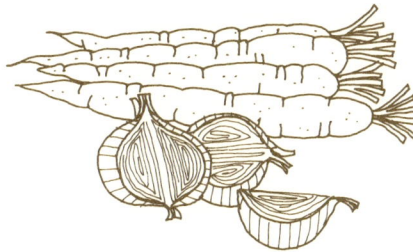

Hearty Potato-Ham Chowder

5 pounds COLORADO potatoes, peeled and cubed (about 15 cups)
3 large onions, finely chopped (about 1 pound)
3 tablespoons instant chicken bouillon granules
2 tablespoons dried marjoram leaves
1 tablespoon dry mustard
1 teaspoon ground black pepper
4 quarts milk, divided
1¼ cups all-purpose flour
1 pound process Swiss cheese, shredded
1½ pounds sodium-reduced ham, diced
½ cup snipped fresh parsley

Cook potatoes and onions in 1 quart water 20 to 30 minutes or until tender. *Do not drain.* Mash slightly. Stir in bouillon granules, marjoram, mustard and pepper. Combine 1 quart (4 cups) milk with flour; whisk to blend until smooth. Add remaining 3 quarts milk, cheese and milk mixture to potato mixture. Cook and stir over medium high heat until slightly thickened and bubbly. Cook and stir 2 minutes longer. Stir in ham and parsley; return to near boiling. Reduce heat; serve hot.

Makes 24 servings

Favorite recipe from **Colorado Potato Administrative Committee**

Country-Style Soups & Stews

Jiffy Chicken & Rice Gumbo

1 (6.9-ounce) package RICE-A-RONI® Chicken Flavor
1 small green bell pepper, coarsely chopped
2 tablespoons margarine or butter
1 pound boneless, skinless chicken breasts, cut into 1-inch pieces
1 (14½-ounce) can diced tomatoes with garlic and onion, undrained
¾ to 1 teaspoon Creole or Cajun seasoning*

½ teaspoon cayenne pepper, ¼ teaspoon dried oregano and ¼ teaspoon dried thyme can be substituted.

1. In large skillet over medium heat, sauté rice-vermicelli mix and bell pepper with margarine until vermicelli is golden brown.

2. Slowly stir in 2¼ cups water, chicken, tomatoes, Creole seasoning and Special Seasonings packet; bring to a boil. Reduce heat to low. Cover; simmer 15 to 20 minutes or until rice is tender.   *Makes 4 servings*

Prep Time: 5 minutes
Cook Time: 30 minutes

Country Vegetable Soup

3 cans (13¾ ounces each) chicken broth
1 cup water
1 package (4½ ounces) creamy chicken, rice and sauce mix
½ teaspoon dried basil
1 bag (16 ounces) BIRDS EYE® frozen Farm Fresh Mixtures Broccoli,
    Green Beans, Pearl Onions and Red Peppers

• Bring broth, water, rice and sauce mix, and basil to boil in large saucepan over high heat.

• Reduce heat to medium. Cook, uncovered, 7 minutes.

• Add vegetables; cook 6 to 7 minutes or until rice and vegetables are tender.
          Makes 4 servings

Prep Time: 5 minutes
Cook Time: 15 minutes

Hearty Minestrone

1 cup dried pinto beans
2 teaspoons olive oil
½ cup chopped red onion
1 clove garlic, minced
3 cans (10 ounces each) no-salt-added whole tomatoes, undrained, chopped
1 medium potato, cut into ½-inch cubes
1 to 1¼ cups coarsely shredded cabbage
1 cup coarsely chopped carrots
1 cup thinly sliced zucchini
⅔ cup coarsely chopped leek
½ cup coarsely chopped celery
2 cups no-salt-added vegetable juice cocktail
2 cups water
1 tablespoon chopped fresh basil *or* 1 teaspoon dried basil leaves
1 teaspoon chopped fresh sage *or* ¼ teaspoon dried sage leaves
2 bay leaves
¼ teaspoon black pepper
1 cup small shell pasta
¼ cup freshly grated Parmesan cheese
1 tablespoon chopped fresh parsley

1. Place dried pinto beans in large glass bowl; cover completely with water. Soak 6 to 8 hours or overnight. Drain beans; discard water.

2. Heat oil in large heavy saucepan or Dutch oven over medium heat. Add onion and garlic; cook and stir until onion is tender.

3. Drain tomatoes, reserving liquid. Add tomatoes to saucepan; mix well. Add pinto beans, cabbage, potato, carrots, zucchini, leek and celery. Stir in vegetable juice, water and reserved tomato liquid. Add basil, sage, bay leaves and black pepper. Bring to a boil over high heat; reduce heat. Cover; simmer 2 hours, stirring occasionally.

4. Add pasta to saucepan 15 minutes before serving. Cook, uncovered, until soup thickens. Remove bay leaves; discard. Top with Parmesan and parsley.

Makes 10 (1½-cup) servings

Lentil Soup

  2 tablespoons olive oil
  1 medium onion, chopped
  1 medium carrot, chopped
  3 quarts (12 cups) chicken broth
  1 jar (1 pound 10 ounces) RAGÚ® Light Pasta sauce
1½ cups uncooked lentils, rinsed and drained
  2 cups coarsely shredded fresh spinach or escarole

1. In 6-quart saucepot, heat olive oil over medium-high heat and cook onion and carrot, stirring occasionally, 4 minutes or until vegetables are golden.

2. Stir in broth, Ragú Pasta Sauce and lentils. Bring to a boil over high heat. Reduce heat to low and simmer, stirring occasionally, 30 minutes or until lentils are tender. Stir in spinach and cook an additional 10 minutes or until spinach is tender.
Makes 3½ quarts soup

Prep Time: 15 minutes
Cook Time: 50 minutes

Home-Style Chili

  1 pound 85% lean ground beef chuck
¾ cup chopped onion
½ teaspoon black pepper
¼ teaspoon salt
  2 cans (14½ ounces each) diced tomatoes with green chilies, undrained
  1 can (16 ounces) chili beans in sauce
  1 cup water
  1 package (1¼ ounces) chili seasoning mix
  1 package (8 ounces) shredded Cheddar cheese (2 cups)

Brown meat in large skillet over medium high heat, stirring to break up meat; drain fat. Add onion, black pepper and salt; cook and stir until onion is tender. Stir in tomatoes with juice, beans with sauce, water and seasoning mix; simmer 25 minutes, stirring occasionally. Divide into bowls; sprinkle with cheese.
Makes about 6 cups

Prep Time: 15 minutes
Cook Time: 30 minutes

Country-Style Soups & Stews

Tomato Soup

    1 tablespoon vegetable oil
    1 cup chopped onion
    2 cloves garlic, coarsely chopped
    ½ cup chopped carrot
    ¼ cup chopped celery
    2 cans (28 ounces each) crushed tomatoes in tomato purée
 3½ cups chicken broth*
    1 tablespoon Worcestershire sauce
    ½ to 1 teaspoon salt
    ½ teaspoon dried thyme leaves
    ¼ to ½ teaspoon black pepper
    2 to 4 drops hot pepper sauce

Substitute 2 cans (10½ ounces each) condensed chicken broth and 1 cup water for 3½ cups chicken broth.

Heat oil in large Dutch oven over medium-high heat. Add onion and garlic; cook and stir 1 to 2 minutes until onion is soft. Add carrot and celery; cook 7 to 9 minutes until tender, stirring frequently. Stir in tomatoes, broth, Worcestershire sauce, salt, thyme, pepper and pepper sauce. Reduce heat to low. Cover; simmer 20 minutes, stirring frequently.

For a smoother soup
Remove from heat. Let cool about 10 minutes. Process soup, in food processor or blender, in small batches until smooth. Return soup to Dutch oven; simmer 3 to 5 minutes until heated through.   *Makes 6 servings*

Hunter-Style Lamb Stew

1 pound boneless American lamb, cut into ¾-inch cubes
2 cloves garlic, minced
¾ cup apple juice or dry red wine
1 cup reduced-sodium chicken broth, divided
½ teaspoon dried rosemary, crushed
¼ teaspoon ground black pepper
⅛ teaspoon ground sage
2 tablespoons all-purpose flour
3 cups cooked linguini
1 to 2 tablespoons chopped fresh parsley

Spray skillet or large saucepan with nonstick cooking spray. Cook and stir lamb cubes and garlic over medium-high heat until lamb is evenly browned. Add apple juice, ½ cup broth, rosemary, pepper and sage. Bring to a boil; reduce heat. Cover and simmer about 1 hour or until lamb is tender. Combine remaining ½ cup broth and flour. Stir into lamb mixture; cook and stir until thickened and bubbly. Cook and stir 1 minute more. Serve lamb mixture over hot cooked linguini. Sprinkle with parsley.

Makes 4 servings

Prep Time: 15 minutes
Cook Time: 1 hour

*Favorite recipe from **American Lamb Council***

Hearty Beef Stew with Noodles

2 tablespoons BERTOLLI® Olive Oil
1 teaspoon finely chopped garlic
1 pound boneless beef sirloin steak, cut into ½-inch cubes
3 cups water
½ cup dry red wine
4 medium new potatoes, quartered
1 large carrot, thinly sliced
1 cup sliced mushrooms
1 cup sliced celery
1 large onion, cut into eighths
1 tablespoon tomato paste
¼ teaspoon dried thyme leaves, crushed
1 bay leaf
1 package LIPTON® Sides Noodles & Sauce—Beef Flavor
1 tablespoon finely chopped parsley
Salt and pepper to taste

In 3-quart saucepan, heat oil over medium heat and cook garlic 30 seconds. Add beef and cook over medium heat, stirring frequently, 2 minutes or until browned. Stir in water, wine, potatoes, carrot, mushrooms, celery, onion, tomato paste, thyme and bay leaf. Bring to a boil, then simmer, stirring occasionally, 30 minutes or until beef is almost tender. Stir in Noodles & Sauce—Beef Flavor and cook 10 minutes or until noodles are tender. Stir in parsley, salt and pepper. Remove bay leaf. *Makes about 4 (2-cup) servings*

Creamy Potato Soup

1 medium onion, finely chopped
1 tablespoon butter or margarine
1¼ pounds DOLE® Yukon Gold or White Potatoes, peeled and diced
2 cups water
3 cups chicken broth
½ teaspoon dried thyme leaves, crushed
½ teaspoon salt
⅛ teaspoon white pepper
½ cup half and half or whipping cream
  Pinch ground nutmeg

• Cook onion in melted butter until tender in large saucepan. Stir in potatoes, water, chicken broth, thyme, salt and pepper. Heat to boiling. Reduce heat to low; cook 10 to 15 minutes or until potatoes are tender. Cool slightly.

• Pour potato mixture into blender or food processor container. Cover; blend until smooth. Stir in half and half and nutmeg. Pour soup into saucepan. Heat until warm (do not boil).   *Makes 5 servings*

Prep Time: 10 minutes
Cook Time: 15 minutes

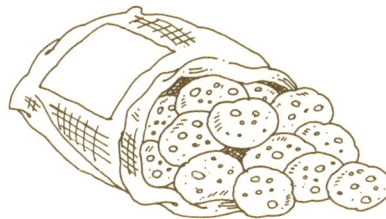

Potato-Corn Chowder

1 cup chopped onion
½ cup chopped green bell pepper
1 teaspoon canola oil
2 cups chopped peeled potatoes
1 can (14½ ounces) fat-free reduced-sodium chicken broth
1 cup frozen corn
1 cup frozen lima beans
1 tablespoon chopped fresh dill *or* 1 teaspoon dried dill weed
¼ teaspoon black pepper
1⅔ cups fat-free (skim) milk, divided
3 tablespoons flour
⅓ cup nonfat dry milk powder
¼ cup chopped fresh parsley

1. Heat oil in large saucepan over medium heat. Add onion and bell pepper; cook and stir until vegetables are tender.

2. Add potatoes, broth, corn, lima beans, dill and black pepper. Bring to a boil over high heat. Reduce heat to medium-low. Cover; simmer 10 to 12 minutes or until potatoes are tender.

3. Combine ⅓ cup skim milk and flour in small bowl. Stir into potato mixture. Stir in remaining 1⅓ cups skim milk and dry milk. Cook and stir over medium heat until mixture boils and thickens. Cook and stir 1 minute more. Ladle chowder into four bowls. Sprinkle with parsley.   *Makes 4 servings*

Hearty 3-Bean & Ham Soup

1 cup chopped onion
1 tablespoon vegetable or olive oil
1 (15-ounce) can each pinto beans, black beans and red kidney beans,
    drained and rinsed
3½ cups water
4 HERB-OX® beef bouillon cubes
1 (14½-ounce) can diced tomatoes
1 cup sliced carrots
⅓ cup chili sauce
3 tablespoons cider vinegar
1 tablespoon firmly packed brown sugar
2 teaspoons Worcestershire sauce
2 teaspoons prepared mustard
1 cup diced ham
2 tablespoons chopped fresh parsley

In large saucepan, sauté onion in oil until golden. Stir in beans and next
9 ingredients. Bring mixture to a boil. Reduce heat, cover and simmer for 25 to
30 minutes or until carrots are tender. Stir in ham and parsley. Ladle into bowls
and serve.

Makes 6 to 8 servings

Prep Time: 15 minutes
Total Time: 1 hour

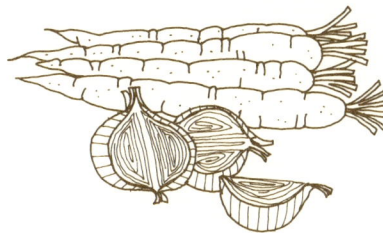

Zesty Chicken & Vegetable Soup

½ pound boneless skinless chicken breasts, cut into very thin strips
1 to 2 tablespoons *Frank's® RedHot®* Original Cayenne Pepper Sauce
4 cups chicken broth
1 package (16 ounces) frozen stir-fry vegetables
1 cup angel hair pasta, broken into 2-inch lengths *or* fine egg noodles
1 green onion, thinly sliced

1. Combine chicken and *Frank's RedHot* Sauce in medium bowl; set aside.

2. Heat broth to boiling in large saucepan over medium-high heat. Add vegetables and pasta; return to boiling. Cook 2 minutes. Stir in chicken mixture and green onion. Cook 1 minute or until chicken is no longer pink.   *Makes 4 to 6 servings*

Tip: For a change of pace, substitute 6 prepared frozen pot stickers for the pasta. Add to broth in step 2 and boil until tender.

Prep Time: 5 minutes
Cook Time: about 8 minutes

Corn and Potato Chowder

2 tablespoons olive oil
½ cup chopped red bell pepper
½ cup chopped green onion
2 cans (12 ounces each) evaporated skim milk
2 cups 1-inch cubed unpeeled red potatoes
2 cups frozen corn
1½ tablespoons MRS. DASH® Classic Italiano Blend
2 tablespoons all-purpose flour

Heat oil in large saucepan. Add red pepper and onion and cook until tender, about 5 minutes. Add milk, potatoes, corn and Classic Italiano Blend; mix well. Bring to a boil; reduce heat and simmer, uncovered, 10 to 12 minutes or until potatoes are tender; stirring frequently. Combine flour and ¼ cup water in small bowl; mix well until smooth. Add to chowder and return to a boil; stir 1 minute. Serve immediately.
Makes 6 servings

Prep Time: 15 minutes
Cook Time: 20 minutes

Creamy Tomato Bisque

½ cup chopped onion
½ cup chopped celery
 1 large clove garlic, crushed
 3 tablespoons butter
¼ cup all-purpose flour
¾ teaspoon basil leaves
½ teaspoon marjoram leaves
½ teaspoon salt
⅛ teaspoon white pepper
 1 can (28 ounces) CONTADINA® Recipe Ready Crushed Tomatoes
 1 can (10.5 ounces) chicken broth
¾ cup water
 1 cup milk, divided

1. Sauté onion, celery, and garlic in butter in medium saucepan. Stir in flour and seasonings.

2. Stir in tomatoes, chicken broth, and water. Heat to boiling.

3. Reduce heat and boil gently, uncovered, 30 minutes.

4. Pour half of tomato mixture and half of milk into blender container. Process until blended. Repeat with remaining soup and milk. Serve warm or cold.

Makes 6½ cups

Microwave Directions: Combine onion, celery, garlic, and butter in 2-quart microwave-safe casserole. Cover loosely. Microwave on HIGH (100%) power for 5 minutes. Mix in flour and seasonings. Stir in tomatoes and juice, chicken broth, and water. Cover again and microwave on HIGH (100%) power for 15 minutes, stirring halfway through cooking time. Process in blender as above.

Chunky Beef and Vegetable Soup

    1 tablespoon corn oil
1¼ pounds beef shank cross cuts
    2 quarts water
    1 cup diced celery
    ½ cup chopped onion
    1 package (10 ounces) frozen mixed vegetables
    1 cup salt-free canned tomatoes, chopped
    1 can (6 ounces) salt-free tomato paste
    1 tablespoon sugar
2½ teaspoons MRS. DASH® All-Purpose Original Blend
    2 teaspoons vinegar
    ¼ cup cold water
    3 tablespoons cornstarch

Heat oil in 3-quart saucepan or Dutch oven. Add beef and brown over medium heat. Add 2 quarts water, celery, and onion. Bring to a boil; reduce heat and simmer for 2 hours. Remove shanks to cool. Stir mixed vegetables, tomatoes, tomato paste, sugar, All-Purpose Original Blend, and vinegar into broth mixture. Simmer for 1 hour. Remove meat from shanks and cut into small chunks: return to vegetable mixture. Combine ¼ cup water and cornstarch in small bowl; mix well until smooth. Stir into vegetable mixture and heat until slightly thickened. *Makes 8 servings*

Prep Time: 20 minutes
Cook Time: 3 hours

Hearty One-Pot Chicken Stew

12 boneless, skinless chicken tenderloins, cut into 1-inch pieces
1 box UNCLE BEN'S CHEF'S RECIPE® Traditional Red Beans & Rice
2¼ cups water
1 can (14½ ounces) diced tomatoes, undrained
3 red potatoes, unpeeled, cut into 1-inch pieces
2 carrots, sliced ½ inch thick
1 onion, cut into 1-inch pieces

In large saucepan, combine chicken, beans & rice, contents of seasoning packet, water, tomatoes, potatoes, carrots and onion. Bring to a boil. Cover; reduce heat and simmer 20 minutes or until vegetables are tender.   *Makes 4 servings*

Minute Minestrone Soup

½ pound turkey sausage, cut into small pieces
2 cloves garlic, crushed
3 cans (14½ ounces each) low-sodium chicken broth
2 cups frozen Italian blend vegetables
1 can (15 ounces) white kidney beans, rinsed and drained
1 can (14½ ounces) Italian stewed tomatoes, undrained
1 cup cooked ditalini or small shell pasta (½ cup uncooked)
3 tablespoons *French's®* Worcestershire Sauce

1. In medium saucepan, stir-fry sausage and garlic 5 minutes or until sausage is cooked; drain. Add broth, vegetables, beans and tomatoes. Heat to boiling. Simmer, uncovered, 5 minutes or until vegetables are crisp-tender.

2. Stir in pasta and Worcestershire. Cook until heated through. Serve with grated cheese and crusty bread, if desired.   *Makes 6 servings*

Prep Time: 10 minutes
Cook Time: about 10 minutes

Beef, Barley & Onion Soup

2 pounds beef stew meat, cut into ½-inch cubes
3 large carrots, cut into ½-inch-thick slices
2 large ribs celery, cut into ½-inch-thick slices
4 cans (14½ ounces each) beef broth
½ teaspoon dried oregano leaves
½ teaspoon salt
¼ teaspoon ground black pepper
½ cup barley
2 cups *French's*® French Fried Onions, divided

Slow Cooker Directions

1. Combine beef, carrots, celery, broth and seasonings in slow cooker. Cover; cook on LOW setting for 7 hours (or on HIGH for 3½ hours) until meat and vegetables are tender.

2. Stir in barley. Cover and cook on LOW setting for 1 hour (or on HIGH for ½ hour) until barley is tender. Stir in *1 cup* French Fried Onions. Spoon soup into serving bowls; sprinkle with remaining onions.   *Makes 8 servings*

Note: Cook times vary depending on type of slow cooker used. Check manufacturer's recommendations for cooking beef and barley.

Prep Time: 20 minutes
Cook Time: 8 hours

Chunky Chili con Carne

2 pounds ground beef
1 cup chopped onion
1 tablespoon minced fresh garlic
1 can (14.5 ounces) HUNT'S® Whole Tomatoes
1 can (14.5 ounces) beef broth
1 can (6 ounces) HUNT'S® Tomato Paste
3 tablespoons GEBHARDT® Chili Powder
1 teaspoon salt
1 teaspoon ground cumin
½ teaspoon dried oregano
½ teaspoon cayenne pepper
1 can (30 ounces) chili beans

In large pot, brown meat with onion and garlic over medium heat; drain. Stir in tomatoes, broth, tomato paste, chili powder, salt, cumin, oregano and cayenne pepper; reduce heat to low and simmer 20 minutes. Stir in beans and simmer additional 10 minutes. *Makes 6 to 8 servings*

Kielbasa and Lentil Stew

1 pound kielbasa or smoked sausage, cut into small cubes
½ head green cabbage, shredded (8 cups)
1 large onion, chopped
4 carrots, shredded
2 cans (19 ounces *each*) lentil soup
1 can (16 ounces) crushed tomatoes in purée, undrained
3 tablespoons *Frank's® RedHot®* Original Cayenne Pepper Sauce

1. Cook and stir sausage in 5-quart saucepot over medium-high heat 3 minutes or until lightly browned. Add vegetables; cook and stir 5 minutes or until tender.

2. Stir in soup, tomatoes and *Frank's RedHot* Sauce. Heat to boiling. Reduce heat to medium-low. Cook, partially covered, 10 minutes or until heated through and flavors are blended. Ladle stew into bowls. *Makes 8 to 10 servings*

Prep Time: 10 minutes
Cook Time: 20 minutes

Harvest Soup

½ pound BOB EVANS® Special Seasonings Roll Sausage
1 large onion, finely chopped
2½ cups chicken broth
2 cups canned pumpkin
2 cups hot milk
1 teaspoon lemon juice
Dash ground nutmeg
Dash ground cinnamon
Salt and black pepper to taste
Chopped fresh parsley

Crumble and cook sausage and onion in large saucepan until sausage is browned. Drain off any drippings. Add broth and bring to a boil. Stir in pumpkin; cover and simmer over low heat 15 to 20 minutes. Add milk, lemon juice, nutmeg, cinnamon, salt and pepper; simmer, uncovered, 5 minutes to blend flavors. Sprinkle with parsley before serving. Refrigerate leftovers.   *Makes 6 to 8 servings*

Irish Stew

3 pounds lamb
3 tablespoons CRISCO® Oil
1 cup carrots cut into cubes
1 cup turnips cut into cubes
1 onion, sliced
1 teaspoon salt
⅛ teaspoon pepper
3 cups potatoes cut into cubes
Additional salt and pepper to taste

Cut lamb into 2-inch square pieces. Heat CRISCO® Oil in Dutch oven. Brown lamb over medium-high heat. Cover with boiling water, and cook slowly for 1½ hours or until tender. Add carrots, turnips, onion, salt and pepper, and cook for 30 minutes. Add potatoes and cook 15 minutes longer. Thicken with a little flour mixed to a paste with cold water. Season with salt and pepper to taste.

Makes 6 to 8 servings

Hearty White Bean Soup

2⅔ cups water, divided
1 can (15 ounces) Great Northern beans or navy beans, rinsed and drained
1 cup chopped carrots
1 cup chopped green bell pepper
1 cup fat-free reduced-sodium chicken broth
½ cup chopped celery
2 tablespoons chopped fresh thyme *or* 2 teaspoons dried thyme leaves
2 tablespoons chopped fresh marjoram *or* 2 teaspoons dried marjoram leaves
½ teaspoon ground cumin
¼ teaspoon black pepper
3 tablespoons all-purpose flour
⅔ cup (about 3 ounces) shredded reduced-fat Swiss or Cheddar cheese

1. Combine 2⅓ cups water, beans, carrots, bell pepper, broth, celery, thyme, marjoram, cumin and black pepper in 3-quart saucepan. Bring to a boil over high heat. Reduce heat to medium-low. Cover; simmer 20 to 25 minutes or until vegetables are tender, stirring occasionally.

2. Combine remaining ⅓ cup water and flour in small bowl. Stir into mixture in saucepan. Cook and stir over medium heat until mixture boils and thickens. Cook and stir 1 minute more. Ladle soup into four bowls. Sprinkle with cheese.

Makes 4 servings

Cozy Casseroles

Green Bean & Turkey Bake

1 can (10¾ ounces) condensed cream of mushroom soup
¾ cup milk
⅛ teaspoon pepper
2 packages (9 ounces each) frozen cut green beans, thawed
2 cups (12 ounces) cubed cooked turkey or chicken
1⅓ cups *French's*® French Fried Onions, divided
1½ cups (6 ounces) shredded Cheddar cheese, divided
3 cups hot mashed potatoes

1. Preheat oven to 375°F. In 3-quart casserole, combine soup, milk and pepper; mix well. Stir in beans, turkey, *⅔ cup* French Fried Onions and *1 cup* cheese. Spoon mashed potatoes on top.

2. Bake, uncovered, 45 minutes or until hot. Sprinkle with remaining *½ cup* cheese and *⅔ cup* onions. Bake 3 minutes or until onions are golden.   *Makes 6 servings*

Microwave Directions: Prepare mixture as above except do not top with potatoes. Cover casserole with vented plastic wrap. Microwave on HIGH 15 minutes or until heated through, stirring halfway through cooking time. Uncover. Top with mashed potatoes, remaining cheese and onions. Microwave on HIGH 2 to 4 minutes. Let stand 5 minutes.

Tip: Two (14½-ounce) cans cut green beans (drained) can be used instead of frozen beans. You can substitute instant mashed potatoes prepared according to package directions for 6 servings.

Prep Time: 10 minutes
Cook Time: 50 minutes

Zesty Chicken & Rice

⅔ cup uncooked regular rice
1⅓ cups *French's*® French Fried Onions, divided
½ teaspoon Italian seasoning
1¾ cups prepared chicken bouillon
4 chicken breast halves, fat trimmed, skinned if desired
⅓ cup bottled Italian salad dressing
1 bag (16 ounces) frozen vegetable combination (broccoli, carrots, water chestnuts, red peppers)

Preheat oven to 400°F. In 13×9-inch baking dish, combine uncooked rice, *⅔ cup* French Fried Onions and Italian seasoning. Pour bouillon over rice mixture. Arrange chicken breasts on top; pour salad dressing over chicken. Bake, covered, at 400°F for 30 minutes. Place vegetables around chicken, covering rice. Bake, uncovered, 20 to 25 minutes or until chicken and rice are done. Top chicken with remaining *⅔ cup* onions; bake, uncovered, 1 to 3 minutes or until onions are golden brown.

Makes 4 servings

Microwave Directions: Reduce bouillon to 1¼ cups. In 12×8-inch microwave-safe dish, combine uncooked rice and bouillon. Cook, covered, on HIGH 5 minutes, stirring rice halfway through cooking time. Stir in vegetables, ⅔ cup onions and Italian seasoning. Arrange chicken over vegetable mixture with meatiest parts toward edges of dish. Pour salad dressing over chicken. Cook, covered, on MEDIUM (50-60%) 15 to 17 minutes or until chicken and rice are done. Rearrange chicken and rotate dish halfway through cooking time. Top chicken with remaining ⅔ cup onions; cook, uncovered, on HIGH 1 minute. Let stand 5 minutes.

Hearty Shepherd's Pie

1½ pounds ground beef
2 cups *French's®* French Fried Onions
1 can (10¾ ounces) condensed tomato soup
2 teaspoons Italian seasoning
1 package (10 ounces) frozen mixed vegetables, thawed
3 cups hot mashed potatoes

1. Preheat oven to 375°F. Cook meat in large oven-proof skillet until browned; drain. Stir in *1 cup* French Fried Onions, soup, *½ cup water,* seasoning and *¼ teaspoon each salt and pepper*.

2. Spoon vegetables over beef mixture. Top with mashed potatoes.

3. Bake 20 minutes or until hot. Sprinkle with remaining *1 cup* onions. Bake 2 minutes or until golden.   *Makes 6 servings*

Prep Time: 10 minutes
Cook Time: 27 minutes

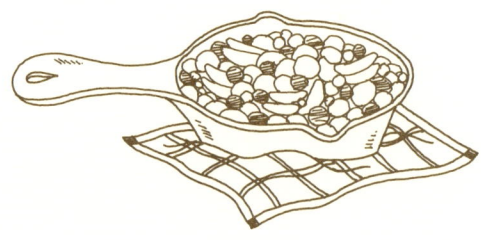

Chicken-Mac Casserole

1½ cups elbow macaroni, cooked in unsalted water and drained
6 slices bacon, fried crisp and crumbled
2 cups (10 ounces) cubed cooked chicken
1⅓ cups *French's*® French Fried Onions, divided
1 can (10¾ ounces) condensed cream of mushroom soup
1 cup sour cream
1 package (10 ounces) frozen chopped spinach, thawed and well drained
⅛ teaspoon garlic powder
1½ cups (6 ounces) shredded Cheddar cheese, divided

Preheat oven to 375°F. Return cooked macaroni to saucepan; stir in bacon, chicken and ⅔ *cup* French Fried Onions. In medium bowl, combine soup, sour cream, spinach, garlic powder and 1 cup Cheddar cheese. Spoon half the macaroni mixture into greased 12×8-inch baking dish; cover with half the spinach mixture. Repeat layers. Bake, covered, at 375°F for 30 minutes or until heated through. Top with remaining cheese and ⅔ *cup* onions. Bake, uncovered, 3 minutes or until onions are golden brown.

Makes 6 to 8 servings

Three Cheese Noodle Bake

1 package (12 ounces) BARILLA® Extra Wide or Wide Egg Noodles
4 tablespoons butter or margarine
4 tablespoons flour
2 cups milk
1 can (14½ ounces) chicken broth
2 cups (8 ounces) shredded Colby-Jack cheese
2 cups (8 ounces) shredded mild Cheddar cheese, divided
½ teaspoon dry mustard
   Salt and pepper
⅛ teaspoon paprika

1. Cook noodles according to package directions; drain. Spray bottom of 13×9×2-inch glass baking dish with nonstick cooking spray.

2. Melt butter in medium saucepan. Stir in flour; cook and stir until smooth. Gradually stir in milk and chicken broth. Cook, stirring constantly, until mixture is smooth and comes to a boil. Reduce heat to low. Add Colby-Jack cheese, 1 cup Cheddar and mustard; cook and stir until cheese melts. Add salt and pepper to taste.

3. Place half of cooked noodles in baking dish. Spoon half of cheese sauce over noodles. Repeat with remaining noodles and cheese sauce. Sprinkle with remaining Cheddar and paprika. Cover with foil and bake 20 to 25 minutes or until hot and bubbly.

Makes 12 servings

Pork-Stuffed Peppers

1 pound ground pork
3 large green peppers
¼ cup raisins
½ cup chopped onion
½ cup chopped carrot
½ cup chopped celery
¼ teaspoon salt
1 cup cooked brown rice
2 tablespoons sunflower kernels
½ cup plain yogurt

Remove tops, seeds and membranes from peppers. Cut in half lengthwise. Cook in boiling salted water 5 minutes; drain.

Soak raisins in water 10 to 15 minutes; drain and set aside. Combine pork, onion, carrot, celery and salt in medium skillet. Cook over low heat until pork is done and vegetables are tender, stirring occasionally. Drain thoroughly. Add rice, sunflower kernels, yogurt and raisins; mix well. Spoon mixture into peppers. Place in 12×8×2-inch baking dish. Bake at 350°F 30 to 35 minutes or until heated through. *Makes 6 servings*

Prep Time: 20 minutes
Cook Time: 30 minutes

Favorite recipe from **National Pork Board**

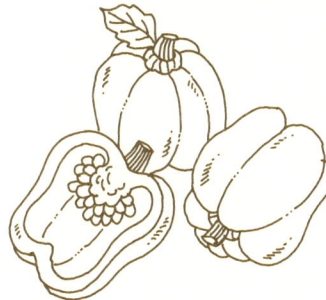

Potato Sausage Casserole

1 pound bulk pork sausage or ground pork
1 can (10¾ ounces) condensed cream of mushroom soup, undiluted
¾ cup milk
½ cup chopped onion
½ teaspoon salt
¼ teaspoon black pepper
3 cups sliced potatoes
1½ cups (6 ounces) shredded Cheddar cheese

1. Preheat oven to 350°F. Spray 1½-quart casserole with nonstick cooking spray; set aside.

2. Cook sausage in large skillet over medium-high heat, stirring to separate, until no longer pink; drain fat.

3. Stir together soup, milk, onion, salt and pepper in medium bowl.

4. Place half of potatoes in prepared casserole. Top with half of soup mixture; top with half of sausage. Repeat layers, ending with sausage.

5. Cover pan with foil. Bake 1¼ to 1½ hours or until potatoes are tender. Uncover; sprinkle with cheese. Return to oven; bake until cheese is melted and bubbly.

Makes 6 servings

Oven Breakfast Hash

2 pounds baking potatoes, unpeeled (5 or 6 medium)
1 pound BOB EVANS® Original Recipe Roll Sausage
1 (12-ounce can) evaporated milk
⅓ cup chopped green onions
1 tablespoon Worcestershire sauce
½ teaspoon salt
¼ teaspoon black pepper
¼ cup dried bread crumbs
1 tablespoon melted butter or margarine
½ teaspoon paprika

Cook potatoes in boiling water until fork-tender. Drain and coarsely chop or mash. Preheat oven to 350°F. Crumble and cook sausage in medium skillet until browned. Drain and transfer to large bowl. Stir in potatoes, milk, green onions, Worcestershire sauce, salt and pepper. Pour into greased 2½- or 3-quart casserole dish. Sprinkle with bread crumbs; drizzle with melted butter. Sprinkle with paprika. Bake, uncovered, 30 to 35 minutes or until casserole bubbles and top is browned. Refrigerate leftovers.

Makes 6 to 8 servings

Breakfast Sausage Casserole

4 cups cubed day-old bread
2 cups (8 ounces) shredded sharp cheddar cheese
2 cans (12 fluid ounces *each*) NESTLÉ® CARNATION® Evaporated Milk
10 large eggs, lightly beaten
1 teaspoon dry mustard
¼ teaspoon onion powder
   Ground black pepper to taste
1 package (16 ounces) fresh breakfast sausage, cooked, drained and crumbled

GREASE 13×9-inch baking dish. Place bread in prepared baking dish. Sprinkle with cheese. Combine evaporated milk, eggs, dry mustard, onion powder and pepper in medium bowl. Pour evenly over bread and cheese. Sprinkle with sausage. Cover; refrigerate overnight.

PREHEAT oven to 325°F.

BAKE for 55 to 60 minutes or until cheese is golden brown. Cover with foil if top browns too quickly.   *Makes 10 to 12 servings*

Heart-y Chicken Pot Pie

3 cups cooked mixed vegetables or frozen thawed vegetables such as peas, carrots and diced potatoes
1 cup cubed cooked, skinless chicken breast
1 can (11¾ ounces) condensed cream of mushroom soup
1⅔ cups biscuit mix
⅔ cup buttermilk
3 tablespoons chopped parsley
¼ teaspoon paprika

1. Preheat oven to 400°F. Lightly spray 9-inch pie plate or other ovenproof casserole. Combine vegetables, chicken and soup. Place filled pie plate in oven.

2. While chicken mixture heats, combine biscuit mix, buttermilk and parsley in medium bowl just until blended. Do not overmix. (Dough will be sticky.) Place dough onto lightly floured surface. With lightly floured hands, gently pat dough into 1-inch-thick disk. Cut 6 biscuits with 2- to 2½-inch biscuit cutter.

3. Remove casserole from oven. Place biscuits on top of chicken mixture and return to oven. Bake about 10 minutes or until biscuits rise and are light gold. *Reduce oven temperature to 350°F.* Continue baking 10 to 15 minutes or until biscuits are done and casserole is heated through. Sprinkle paprika over biscuits during the last five minutes of baking.

Makes 6 servings

Manicotti Florentine

12 manicotti shells
1 pound 85% lean ground beef
1 medium onion, finely chopped
1 teaspoon minced garlic
½ teaspoon salt
½ teaspoon dried basil
½ teaspoon dried thyme
½ teaspoon dried oregano
⅛ teaspoon freshly ground black pepper
1 package (10 ounces) frozen chopped spinach, thawed and squeezed dry
1 packet (1.6 ounces) Alfredo sauce mix prepared according to package directions, divided
1 jar (26 ounces) prepared marinara sauce
½ cup shredded fresh Parmesan cheese

Cook manicotti shells according to package directions.

In a large skillet over medium high heat, brown beef, onion and garlic, crumbling beef into small pieces. Remove from heat and drain. Add salt, basil, thyme, oregano and pepper. Mix in spinach and 1 cup of prepared Alfredo sauce. Spoon mixture into a large resealable plastic bag. Snip off one bottom corner of the bag and pipe mixture into manicotti shells. Place manicotti shells in a greased shallow 2-quart baking dish. Pour marinara sauce over the top; drizzle remaining Alfredo sauce over and sprinkle with Parmesan cheese.

Bake in a preheated 350°F oven 20 minutes or until heated through.

Makes 5 servings

*Favorite recipe from **North Dakota Wheat Commission***

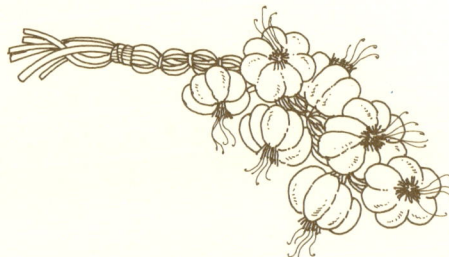

Chicken Tetrazzini

1 can (10¾ ounces) condensed cream of mushroom soup
1⅓ cups *French's*® French Fried Onions, divided
1¼ cups milk
1 cup (4 ounces) shredded Monterey Jack cheese, divided
2 tablespoons minced parsley
¼ teaspoon dried oregano leaves
¼ teaspoon garlic powder
4 cups cooked spaghetti (8 ounces uncooked)
2 cups (10 ounces) finely cubed cooked chicken
1 package (10 ounces) frozen peas and carrots, thawed

1. Preheat oven to 350°F. In large bowl, combine soup, ⅔ cup French Fried Onions, milk, ½ cup cheese, parsley, oregano and garlic powder. Stir in spaghetti, chicken and vegetables. Pour into lightly greased 2-quart baking dish.

2. Bake, uncovered, 30 minutes or until heated through. Stir. Top with remaining ⅔ cup onions and ½ cup cheese. Bake 5 minutes or until onions are golden.

Makes 6 servings

Prep Time: 5 minutes
Cook Time: 35 minutes

Chili Meatloaf and Potato Bake

1½ pounds ground turkey
1⅓ cups *French's*® French Fried Onions, divided
¾ cup salsa
1 egg, beaten
1 tablespoon chili powder
½ teaspoon salt
¼ teaspoon ground black pepper
2 cups prepared hot mashed potatoes
2 cups (8 ounces) shredded taco blend cheese, divided

1. Preheat oven to 375°F. Combine ground turkey, *⅔ cup* French Fried Onions, salsa, egg, chili powder, salt and pepper until blended. Press turkey mixture into 9-inch square baking dish.

2. Bake 25 minutes or until turkey is cooked through and juices run clear. Drain off fat.

3. Combine potatoes and 1 cup cheese. Spread evenly over meatloaf. Sprinkle with remaining cheese and onions; bake 5 minutes or until cheese is melted and onions are golden. *Makes 6 servings*

Tip: To make in a hurry, prepare instant mashed potatoes for 4 servings.

Variation: For added Cheddar flavor, substitute *French's*® **Cheddar French Fried Onions** for the original flavor.

Prep Time: 15 minutes
Cook Time: 30 minutes

Potato Bacon Casserole

4 cups frozen shredded hash brown potatoes
½ cup finely chopped onion
8 ounces bacon or turkey bacon, cooked and crumbled*
1 cup (4 ounces) shredded cheddar cheese
1 can (12 fluid ounces) NESTLÉ® CARNATION® Evaporated Milk
    or NESTLÉ® CARNATION® Evaporated Lowfat Milk
1 large egg, lightly beaten or ¼ cup egg substitute
1½ teaspoons seasoned salt

Can substitute with 1 package (2.1 ounces) precooked bacon slices, cut into small pieces.

PREHEAT oven to 350°F. Grease 8-inch square baking dish.

LAYER ½ potatoes, ½ onion, ½ bacon and ½ cheese in prepared baking dish; repeat layers. Combine evaporated milk, egg and seasoned salt in small bowl. Pour evenly over potato mixture; cover.

BAKE for 55 to 60 minutes. Uncover; bake for an additional 5 minutes. Let stand for 10 to 15 minutes before serving.   *Makes 6 servings*

Quick Chopped Chicken and Artichoke Casserole

4 boneless, skinless chicken breast halves
1 can (13¾ ounces) quartered, water-packed artichoke hearts, drained
1 can (8 ounces) sliced water chestnuts, drained
1 can (2 ounces) diced pimento
1 cup mayonnaise
⅓ cup minced onion
¼ teaspoon pepper
½ cup grated Parmesan cheese
⅓ cup dry seasoned bread crumbs

In medium saucepan, cover chicken with cold water. Bring to boil; reduce to low. Heat and simmer, covered, about 7 minutes. Turn off heat; remove cover and let chicken cool in the water for 10 minutes.

While chicken is cooling, stir together artichoke hearts, water chestnuts, pimento, mayonnaise, onion and pepper in medium bowl. In small bowl, stir together Parmesan cheese and bread crumbs. Stir half the crumb mixture into artichoke mixture. Set remaining bread crumbs aside.

Preheat oven to 400°F.

Dice chicken and stir into artichoke mixture. Spoon into 1½ quart casserole and smooth top. Sprinkle with reserved crumbs. Bake about 35 minutes, until golden brown and heated through.

Makes 4 servings

Tip: To freeze, cover tightly with plastic wrap and freeze until needed. To thaw, transfer from freezer to refrigerator 12 to 24 hours in advance. Bake in preheated 400°F. oven for about 40 minutes, until golden brown and heated through.

*Favorite recipe from **National Chicken Council***

Stuffed Peppers

1 bag SUCCESS® Rice
   Water
4 medium green bell peppers, seeded and halved
1 pound ground turkey *or* 90% lean ground beef
1 can (14½ ounces) stewed tomatoes
1 egg, slightly beaten
1 envelope (0.8 ounce) dry onion soup mix
⅛ teaspoon cayenne pepper
1 cup (4 ounces) shredded Monterey Jack cheese

Prepare rice according to package directions.

Place green peppers in large saucepan or Dutch oven. Add enough water to cover. Bring to a boil over medium-high heat. Reduce heat to low; cover. Steam 5 minutes. Remove peppers from pan; drain.

Brown ground turkey in large skillet, stirring occasionally to separate turkey; drain. Stir in rice, tomatoes, egg, soup mix and cayenne pepper. Add cheese; mix lightly. Spoon turkey mixture into peppers. Place in shallow baking dish; cover. Bake until peppers are crisp-tender and filling is thoroughly heated, about 20 minutes.

Makes 8 servings

Tomato-Bread Casserole

½ pound loaf French bread, sliced

3 tablespoons butter or margarine, softened

1½ pounds tomatoes, thinly sliced

1 cup lowfat cottage or ricotta cheese

1 can (14½ ounces) diced tomatoes, drained (reserving liquid)

¾ teaspoon LAWRY'S® Seasoned Salt

½ teaspoon oregano

¼ cup olive oil

¾ teaspoon LAWRY'S® Garlic Powder With Parsley

½ cup shredded Parmesan cheese

¼ cup chopped parsley (garnish)

Spread bread slices with butter; cut into large cubes. Arrange on baking sheet. Toast in 350°F oven until golden. Place ½ of cubes in greased 13×9×2-inch baking dish. Top bread cubes with ½ of fresh tomato slices, ½ of cottage cheese, ½ of canned tomatoes, ½ reserved tomato liquid, ½ of Seasoned Salt, ½ of oregano, ½ of oil, and Garlic Powder with Parsley. Layer again ending with oil. Sprinkle on Parmesan cheese. Cover and bake in 350°F oven for 40 minutes. Uncover and bake 5 minutes longer to brown top. Garnish with parsley. *Makes 6 to 8 servings*

Meal Idea: Serve with marinated mushrooms.

Prep Time: 15 minutes
Cook Time: 45 minutes

Rice & Sausage Casserole

1 cup uncooked rice
1 pound BOB EVANS® Zesty Hot or Special Seasonings Roll Sausage
2 tablespoons butter or margarine
1 cup chopped celery
1 large onion, chopped
¼ cup *each* chopped red and green bell peppers
1 (10½-ounce) can condensed cream of mushroom soup
1 cup milk
    Salt and black pepper to taste
½ cup (2 ounces) shredded longhorn or colby cheese

Cook rice according to package directions; transfer to large bowl. Preheat oven to 350°F. Crumble sausage into medium skillet. Cook over medium heat until lightly browned, stirring occasionally. Remove sausage to paper towels; set aside. Drain off any drippings and wipe skillet clean with paper towels. Stir sausage into cooked rice. Melt butter in same skillet over medium-high heat until hot. Add celery, onion and bell peppers; cook and stir until tender. Stir into rice and sausage mixture. Stir in soup, milk, salt and black pepper; mix well. Spoon mixture into lightly greased 2-quart baking dish. Sprinkle with cheese. Bake, uncovered, 40 minutes or until heated through. Serve hot. Refrigerate leftovers.   *Makes 6 servings*

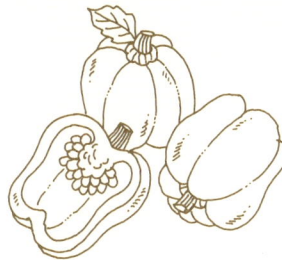

Chicken Broccoli Rice Casserole

3 cups cooked long grain rice

4 boneless skinless chicken breasts (about 1 pound), cooked and
   cut into bite-size pieces

1½ pounds broccoli, steamed until tender and cut into bite-size pieces

2 cans (10¾ ounces each) condensed cream of celery soup, undiluted

¾ cup mayonnaise

½ cup milk

2 teaspoons curry powder

3 cups (12 ounces) shredded sharp Cheddar cheese

1. Preheat oven to 350°F.

2. Butter 13×9-inch baking dish. Place cooked rice evenly into dish. Arrange chicken and broccoli on top. Mix together soup, mayonnaise, milk and curry powder in medium bowl; pour over chicken and broccoli. Top with cheese.

3. Cover loosely with foil and bake 45 minutes or until cheese melts and casserole is heated through.

Makes 4 to 6 servings

Ham with Spring Vegetables

1 can (10¾ ounces) condensed cream of celery soup, undiluted
¾ cup uncooked rice
1 tablespoon butter or margarine
1 to 1½ pounds HILLSHIRE FARM® Ham, cut into bite-size pieces
1 package (10 ounces) frozen mixed vegetables
1 can (4 ounces) sliced mushrooms, drained
1 cup (4 ounces) shredded Swiss cheese

Preheat oven to 350°F.

Combine soup, rice, ¾ cup water and butter in large skillet over medium heat. Bring mixture to a boil; reduce heat and simmer 5 minutes. Combine rice mixture with Ham, vegetables and mushrooms in medium casserole; sprinkle top with cheese. Bake, covered, 20 to 25 minutes or until rice is cooked.

Makes 4 servings

Crunchy Tuna Casserole

6 ounces medium noodles or macaroni, cooked and drained
1 can (10¾ ounces) condensed cream of chicken soup, undiluted
1 can (6 ounces) tuna, drained and flaked
1 cup (4 ounces) shredded sharp Cheddar cheese
½ cup sliced celery
½ cup milk
¼ cup mayonnaise
1 can (4 ounces) sliced water chestnuts, drained
1 jar (2 ounces) chopped pimientos, drained
½ teaspoon salt
    Dash pepper
    Pinch celery seeds

Preheat oven to 425°F. Spray 2-quart casserole with nonstick cooking spray. Combine all ingredients in prepared casserole. Bake 25 minutes or until hot and bubbly.

Makes 6 servings

Pennsylvania Dutch Chicken Bake

1 package (about 1¾ pounds) PERDUE® Fresh Skinless Chicken Thighs
  Salt and pepper to taste
1 to 2 tablespoons canola oil
1 can (14 to 16 ounces) sauerkraut, undrained
1 can (14 to 15 ounces) whole onions, drained
1 tart red apple, unpeeled and sliced
6 to 8 dried whole apricots
½ cup raisins
¼ cup brown sugar, or to taste

Preheat oven to 350°F. Season thighs with salt and pepper. In large nonstick skillet over medium-high heat, heat oil. Cook thighs 6 to 8 minutes per side until browned. Meanwhile, in 12×9-inch shallow baking dish, mix sauerkraut, onions, apple, apricots, raisins and brown sugar until blended. Arrange thighs in sauerkraut mixture. Cover and bake 30 to 40 minutes or until chicken is cooked through and a meat thermometer inserted in thickest part of thigh registers 180°F.

Makes 6 servings

Variation: If desired, substitute other fresh or dried fruit in this recipe, such as pears or pitted prunes.

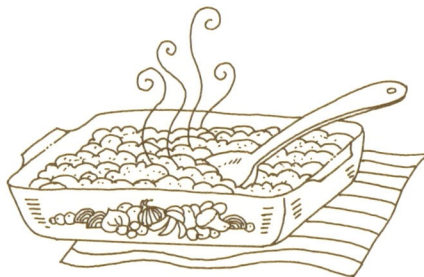

Sausage-Chicken Creole

1 can (14½ ounces) whole tomatoes, undrained and cut up
½ cup uncooked regular rice
½ cup hot water
2 teaspoons *Frank's® RedHot®* Original Cayenne Pepper Sauce
¼ teaspoon garlic powder
¼ teaspoon dried oregano, crumbled
1 bag (16 ounces) frozen vegetable combination (broccoli, corn, red pepper), thawed and drained
1⅓ cups *French's®* French Fried Onions, divided
4 chicken thighs, skinned
½ pound link Italian sausage, quartered and cooked*
1 can (8 ounces) tomato sauce

To cook sausage, simmer in water to cover until done. Or, place in microwave-safe dish and cook, covered, on HIGH 3 minutes or until done.

Preheat oven to 375°F. In 12×8-inch baking dish, combine tomatoes, uncooked rice, hot water, **Frank's RedHot** Sauce and seasonings. Bake, covered, at 375°F for 10 minutes. Stir vegetables and ⅔ cup French Fried Onions into rice mixture; top with chicken and cooked sausage. Pour tomato sauce over chicken and sausage. Bake, covered, at 375°F for 40 minutes or until chicken is done. Top chicken with remaining ⅔ cup onions; bake, uncovered, 3 minutes or until onions are golden brown.
Makes 4 servings

Cozy Casseroles

Mom's Best Chicken Tetrazzini

8 ounces uncooked thin noodles or vermicelli
2 tablespoons butter
8 ounces fresh mushrooms, sliced
¼ cup chopped green onions
1 can (about 14 ounces) chicken broth
1 cup half-and-half, divided
2 tablespoons dry sherry
¼ cup all-purpose flour
½ teaspoon salt
¼ teaspoon ground nutmeg
⅛ teaspoon white pepper
1 jar (2 ounces) chopped pimiento, drained
½ cup (4 ounces) grated Parmesan cheese, divided
½ cup sour cream
2 cups cubed cooked chicken

1. Preheat oven to 350°F. Cook noodles according to package directions. Drain; set aside.

2. Melt butter in large nonstick skillet over medium-high heat. Add mushrooms and onions; cook and stir until onions are tender. Add chicken broth, ½ cup half-and-half and sherry to onion mixture. Pour remaining ½ cup half-and-half into small jar with tight-fitting lid; add flour, salt, nutmeg and pepper. Shake well. Slowly stir flour mixture into skillet. Bring to a boil; cook 1 minute. Reduce heat; stir in pimiento and ¼ cup Parmesan cheese. Stir in sour cream; blend well. Add chicken and noodles; mix well.

3. Spray 1½-quart casserole with nonstick cooking spray. Spread mixture evenly into prepared casserole. Sprinkle with remaining ¼ cup Parmesan cheese. Bake 30 to 35 minutes or until hot.

Makes 6 servings

Tasty Turkey Divan

1 can (10¾ ounces) condensed cream of mushroom soup
¾ cup milk
2 cups cubed cooked turkey
1 package (10 ounces) frozen broccoli florets, thawed
1⅓ cups *French's*® French Fried Onions, divided
4 to 5 slices buttered, toasted white bread
1 cup grated Parmesan cheese

1. Preheat oven to 350°F. Combine soup and milk in medium bowl; stir in turkey, broccoli and *⅔ cup* French Fried Onions.

2. Place toast slices in bottom of greased 2-quart shallow baking dish, cutting to fit if necessary. Spoon turkey mixture on top.

3. Bake 25 minutes or until mixture is heated through. Sprinkle with cheese and remaining onions; bake 5 minutes or until cheese is melted and onions are golden.

Makes 6 servings

Prep Time: 10 minutes
Cook Time: 30 minutes

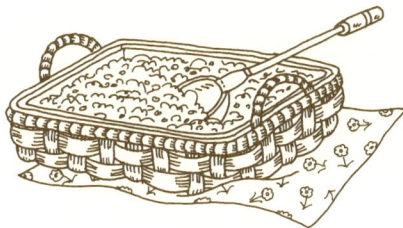

Turkey Pot Pie

1 (1-pound) package frozen vegetables for stew, cooked according
    to package directions
1 cup frozen peas, cooked according to package directions
2 cups COOKED TURKEY from a TURKEY ROAST, cut into ½-inch cubes
    (cook roast according to package directions)*
1 (12-ounce) jar non-fat turkey gravy
1 tablespoon dried parsley
1 teaspoon dried thyme
1 teaspoon dried rosemary
½ teaspoon salt
¼ teaspoon pepper
1 refrigerated pie crust dough (brought to room temperature)

Leftover cooked turkey can be substituted for the pre-packaged turkey roast.

1. Drain any cooking liquid from stew vegetables and peas.

2. Add turkey cubes, gravy, parsley, thyme, rosemary, salt and pepper to vegetables in oven-safe, 2-quart cooking dish.

3. Unfold pie crust dough and place on top of dish, trimming edges to approximately 1 inch larger than dish; secure dough edges to dish. Make several 1-inch slits on crust to allow steam to escape.

4. Bake in preheated 400°F oven for 25 to 30 minutes or until crust is brown and mixture is hot and bubbly.
        Makes 5 servings

Favorite recipe from **National Turkey Federation**

Zesty Cheddar Casserole

2 packages (1½ ounces each) 4-cheese pasta sauce mix
2 cups milk
1 cup finely chopped celery
½ cup chopped onion
3 to 4 tablespoons *Frank's® RedHot®* Original Cayenne Pepper Sauce
1 bag (16 ounces) frozen vegetable combination such as broccoli,
    corn and red bell pepper
3 cups cooked diced chicken
6 slices crisply cooked bacon, crumbled
1½ cups (6 ounces) shredded Cheddar cheese, divided
1 package (7½ ounces) refrigerated buttermilk biscuits

1. Preheat oven to 375°F. Prepare sauce mix according to package directions using milk, 1 cup water and omitting butter in 3-quart saucepan. Add celery, onion and *Frank's RedHot* Sauce. Cook and stir 1 minute.

2. Stir in vegetable combination, chicken, bacon and 1 cup cheese. Spoon into greased 3-quart casserole; cover. Bake 30 minutes; stir. Cut biscuits in half crosswise; arrange around edge of casserole. Sprinkle remaining ½ cup cheese over biscuits.

3. Bake, uncovered, 15 minutes or until biscuits are golden brown.

Makes 8 servings

Prep Time: 25 minutes
Cook Time: 50 minutes

Easy Beef Lasagna

 1 pound ground beef
 1 jar (1 pound 10 ounces) RAGÚ® Old World Style® Pasta Sauce
 1 container (15 ounces) ricotta cheese
 2 cups shredded mozzarella cheese (about 8 ounces)
 ½ cup grated Parmesan cheese, divided
 2 eggs
 12 lasagna noodles, cooked and drained

1. Preheat oven to 375°F. In 12-inch skillet, brown ground beef; drain. Stir in Ragú Pasta Sauce; heat through.

2. In large bowl, combine ricotta cheese, mozzarella cheese, ¼ cup Parmesan cheese and eggs.

3. In 13×9-inch baking dish, evenly spread 1 cup meat sauce. Arrange 4 lasagna noodles lengthwise over sauce, then 1 cup meat sauce and ½ of the ricotta cheese mixture; repeat, ending with sauce. Cover with aluminum foil and bake 30 minutes. Sprinkle with remaining ¼ cup Parmesan cheese. Bake uncovered 5 minutes. Let stand 10 minutes before serving.   *Makes 10 servings*

Prep Time: 30 minutes
Cook Time: 35 minutes

Escalloped Chicken

10 slices white bread, cubed
1½ cups cracker or dry bread crumbs, divided
4 cups cubed cooked chicken
3 cups chicken broth
1 cup chopped onion
1 cup chopped celery
1 can (8 ounces) sliced mushrooms, drained
1 jar (about 4 ounces) pimientos, diced
3 eggs, lightly beaten
Salt and black pepper
1 tablespoon margarine

1. Preheat oven to 350°F.

2. Combine bread cubes and 1 cup cracker crumbs in large mixing bowl. Add chicken, broth, onion, celery, mushrooms, pimientos and eggs; mix well. Season with salt and pepper; spoon into 2½-quart casserole.

3. Melt margarine in small saucepan. Add remaining ½ cup cracker crumbs and brown, stirring occasionally. Sprinkle crumbs over casserole.

4. Bake 1 hour or until hot and bubbly.

Makes 6 servings

Turkey Tetrazini Casserole

6 ounces egg noodles
2 HERB-OX® chicken flavored instant low sodium bouillon packets
1 (15-ounce) can evaporated skim milk
¼ cup all-purpose flour
⅛ teaspoon ground nutmeg
2 cups diced, cooked turkey
6 green onions, sliced
1 (2-ounce) jar chopped pimentos
¼ cup grated Parmesan cheese, divided
2 tablespoons slivered almonds, toasted

Preheat oven to 350°F. Cook egg noodles as package directs. Meanwhile, in large saucepan, over medium-high heat, bring bouillon, evaporated milk, flour and nutmeg to a boil. Cook, stirring until thick and bubbly about 2 minutes. Add turkey, cooked noodles, green onion, pimentos and 2 tablespoons grated Parmesan cheese. Transfer turkey mixture to a lightly greased 2-quart casserole dish. Sprinkle with remaining 2 tablespoons cheese and almonds. Bake 20 to 25 minutes or until hot and bubbly.

Makes 6 servings

Prep Time: 20 minutes
Total Time: 45 minutes

Savory Pork Chop Supper

6 medium potatoes, thinly sliced (about 5 cups)
1⅓ cups *French's®* French Fried Onions, divided
1 jar (2 ounces) sliced mushrooms, drained
2 tablespoons butter or margarine
¼ cup soy sauce
1½ teaspoons ground mustard
½ teaspoon *Frank's® RedHot®* Original Cayenne Pepper Sauce
⅛ teaspoon garlic powder
1 tablespoon vegetable oil
6 pork chops, ½ to ¾ inch thick

Preheat oven to 350°F. In 12×8-inch baking dish, layer half the potatoes and ⅔ *cup* French Fried Onions. Top with mushrooms and remaining potatoes. In small saucepan, melt butter; stir in soy sauce, mustard, *Frank's RedHot* Sauce and garlic powder. Brush half the soy sauce mixture over potatoes. In large skillet, heat oil. Brown pork chops on both sides; drain. Arrange chops over potatoes and brush with remaining soy sauce mixture. Bake, covered, at 350°F for 1 hour. Bake, uncovered, 15 minutes or until pork chops and potatoes are done. Top chops with remaining ⅔ *cup* onions; bake, uncovered, 5 minutes or until onions are golden brown.   *Makes 4 to 6 servings*

Tuna-Macaroni Casserole

1 cup mayonnaise
1 cup (4 ounces) shredded Swiss cheese
½ cup milk
¼ cup chopped onion
¼ cup chopped sweet red bell pepper or pimiento
⅛ teaspoon black pepper
2 cans (7 ounces each) tuna, drained and flaked
1 package (about 10 ounces) frozen peas
2 cups shell pasta or elbow macaroni, cooked and drained
½ cup dry bread crumbs (optional)
2 tablespoons melted butter or corn oil (optional)

1. Preheat oven to 350°F.

2. Stir together mayonnaise, cheese, milk, onion, red pepper and black pepper in large bowl. Add tuna, peas and macaroni, toss to coat well.

3. Spoon into 2-quart casserole. If desired, mix bread crumbs with butter in small bowl and sprinkle on top. Bake 30 to 40 minutes or until heated through.

Makes 6 servings

Quick Chicken Stew with Biscuits

1 can (10¾ ounces) cream of roasted chicken soup with savory herbs
1 bag (16 ounces) frozen Southwestern or Mexican-style vegetables
1 package (10 ounces) PERDUE® SHORT CUTS® Fully Cooked Carved
    Chicken Breast, Honey Roasted
1 package (8 ounces) shredded Mexican cheese or Monterey Jack cheese
    (2 cups), divided
1½ cups buttermilk baking mix
½ cup milk

Preheat oven to 425°F. In lightly greased 12×8-inch baking dish, combine soup
and ½ soup can water. Stir in vegetables, chicken and 1 cup cheese. Cover and
bake 20 minutes. Meanwhile, in mixing bowl, combine baking mix, remaining
1 cup cheese and milk; stir with fork until all of baking mix is moistened. Spoon
baking mix on top of chicken mixture. Bake 15 to 20 minutes, until biscuit topping
is golden brown and sauce is hot and bubbly.   *Makes 4 to 6 servings*

Prep Time: 10 minutes
Cook Time: 35 to 40 minutes

Pork with Savory Apple Stuffing

1 package (6 ounces) corn bread stuffing mix
1 can (14½ ounces) chicken broth
1 small apple, peeled, cored and chopped
¼ cup chopped celery
1⅓ cups *French's*® French Fried Onions, divided
4 boneless pork chops, ¾ inch thick (about 1 pound)
½ cup peach-apricot sweet & sour sauce
1 tablespoon *French's*® Honey Dijon Mustard

1. Preheat oven to 375°F. Combine stuffing mix, broth, apple, celery and ⅔ *cup* French Fried Onions in large bowl. Spoon into bottom of greased shallow 2-quart baking dish. Arrange chops on top of stuffing.

2. Combine sweet & sour sauce with mustard in small bowl. Pour over pork. Bake 40 minutes or until pork is no longer pink in center.

3. Sprinkle with remaining onions. Bake 5 minutes or until onions are golden.

Makes 4 servings

Prep Time: 10 minutes
Cook Time: 45 minutes

Chicken Noodle Casserole

1 package (12 ounces) wide egg noodles
1 can (10¾ ounces) condensed cream of mushroom soup, undiluted
1 can (10¾ ounces) condensed cream of chicken soup, undiluted
1 can (6 ounces) cooked white chicken
½ cup milk
½ cup shredded Cheddar-Jack cheese
½ cup sour cream
1 cup dry bread crumbs

1. Prepare egg noodles as directed on package. Drain well; place in large saucepan.

2. Add soups, chicken, milk, cheese and sour cream. Cook and stir over medium heat until heated through. Pour into 13×9-inch casserole; top with bread crumbs.

3. Place casserole under broiler for 5 to 10 minutes or until bread crumbs are crispy.

Makes 4 to 6 servings

Potato-Ham Scallop

2 cups cubed HILLSHIRE FARM® Ham
6 potatoes, peeled and thinly sliced
¼ cup chopped onion
⅓ cup all-purpose flour
   Salt and black pepper to taste
2 cups milk
3 tablespoons bread crumbs
1 tablespoon butter or margarine, melted

Preheat oven to 350°F.

Place ½ of Ham in medium casserole. Cover with ½ of potatoes and ½ of onion. Sift ½ of flour over onions; sprinkle with salt and pepper. Repeat layers with remaining ham, potatoes, onion, flour, salt and pepper. Pour milk over casserole. Bake, covered, 1¼ hours. Combine bread crumbs and butter in small bowl; sprinkle over top of casserole. Bake, uncovered, 15 minutes or until topping is golden brown.

Makes 6 servings

Chili Cornbread Casserole

1 pound ground beef
1 medium onion, chopped
1 jar (1 pound) RAGÚ® Cheese Creations!® Double Cheddar Sauce
1 can (19 ounces) red kidney beans, rinsed and drained
1 can (8¾ ounces) whole kernel corn, drained
2 to 3 teaspoons chili powder
1 package (12 ounces) cornbread mix

Preheat oven to 400°F. In 12-inch skillet, brown ground beef and onion over medium-high heat; drain. Stir in Ragú Cheese Creations! Sauce, beans, corn and chili powder.

Meanwhile, prepare cornbread mix according to package directions. Do not bake.

In ungreased 2-quart baking dish, spread ground beef mixture. Top with cornbread mixture. Bake uncovered 20 minutes or until toothpick inserted in center of cornbread comes out clean and top is golden.   *Makes 6 servings*

Prep Time: 10 minutes
Cook Time: 20 minutes

Supper-Time Favorites

Oven-Barbecued Ribs

¼ cup CRISCO® Oil
3 to 4 pounds pork spareribs, cut into serving-size pieces
½ cup finely diced onion
⅓ cup finely diced celery
¼ cup finely grated carrot
⅓ cup ketchup
¼ cup packed brown sugar
1 tablespoon prepared mustard
1½ teaspoons chili powder
½ teaspoon salt
¼ teaspoon cayenne

Preheat oven to 350°F.

Heat CRISCO® Oil in large skillet. Add ribs. Brown over medium-high heat. Remove ribs from skillet; set aside. Discard drippings, reserving 2 tablespoons in skillet. Arrange ribs in 13×9-inch baking dish. Cover dish with aluminum foil. Bake 1 hour.

Meanwhile, heat 2 tablespoons reserved drippings in skillet. Add onion, celery and carrot. Cook and stir over moderate heat until tender. Stir in remaining ingredients. Simmer, stirring occasionally, about 5 minutes.

Drain ribs. Baste generously with sauce. Cover with foil. Bake 30 to 60 minutes or until tender.   *Makes 4 servings*

Supper-Time Favorites

Tuna Skillet Supper

1 package (8 ounces) cream cheese, softened
1 cup milk
1 packet (1 ounce) HIDDEN VALLEY® The Original Ranch® Salad Dressing
    & Seasoning Mix
8 ounces uncooked spiral egg noodles
2 cups frozen petite peas, thawed
2 cans (6 ounces each) tuna or shrimp, drained

In a food processor fitted with a metal blade, blend cream cheese, milk and salad dressing & seasoning mix until smooth.

Cook pasta according to package directions; drain and combine with peas and tuna in a large skillet. Stir dressing mixture into pasta. Cook over low heat until mixture is hot.
Makes 4 to 6 servings

The Original Ranch® Crispy Chicken

¼ cup unseasoned bread crumbs or corn flake crumbs
1 packet (1 ounce) HIDDEN VALLEY® The Original Ranch® Salad Dressing
    & Seasoning Mix
6 bone-in chicken pieces

Combine bread crumbs and salad dressing & seasoning mix in a resealable plastic bag. Add chicken pieces; seal bag. Shake to coat chicken. Bake chicken on an ungreased baking sheet at 375°F. for 50 minutes or until no longer pink in center and juices run clear.
Makes 4 to 6 servings

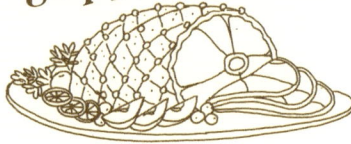

Supper-Time Favorites

Old-Fashioned Cabbage Rolls

½ pound ground beef
½ pound ground veal
½ pound ground pork
1 small onion, chopped
2 eggs, lightly beaten
½ cup dry bread crumbs
1 teaspoon salt
1 teaspoon molasses
¼ teaspoon ground ginger
¼ teaspoon ground nutmeg
¼ teaspoon ground allspice
1 large head cabbage, separated into leaves
3 cups boiling water
¼ cup butter or margarine
½ cup milk, or more as needed
1 tablespoon cornstarch

1. Combine meats and onion in large bowl. Combine eggs, bread crumbs, salt, molasses, ginger, nutmeg and allspice in medium bowl; mix well. Add to meat mixture; stir until well blended.

2. Drop cabbage leaves into boiling water for 3 minutes. Remove with slotted spoon, reserving ½ cup of boiling liquid.

3. Preheat oven to 375°F. Place about 2 tablespoons of meat mixture about 1 inch from stem end of each leaf. Fold sides in and roll up, fastening with toothpicks, if necessary.

4. Heat butter in large skillet over medium-high heat. Add cabbage rolls (3 or 4 at a time) to skillet and brown on all sides. Arrange rolls, seam side down, in single layer in casserole. Combine reserved 1/2 cup boiling liquid with butter remaining in skillet; pour over cabbage rolls.

5. Bake 1 hour. Remove and carefully drain accumulated pan juices into measuring cup. Return cabbage rolls to oven. Add enough milk to pan juices to equal 1 cup.

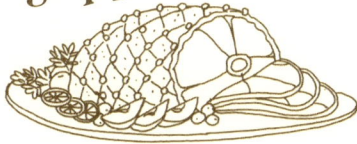 
6. Pour milk mixture into small saucepan. Stir in cornstarch; bring to a boil, stirring constantly until sauce is thickened. Pour over cabbage rolls. Bake 15 minutes more or until sauce is browned and cabbage is very tender.

Makes 8 servings

Skillet Chicken Alfredo

4 boneless, skinless chicken breast halves (about 1¼ pounds)
1 egg, lightly beaten
½ cup Italian seasoned dry bread crumbs
2 tablespoons olive oil
1 jar (1 pound) RAGÚ® Cheese Creations!® Classic Alfredo Sauce
1 small tomato, cut into 4 slices
4 slices mozzarella cheese *or* ½ cup shredded mozzarella cheese
    (about 2 ounces)

1. Dip chicken in egg, then bread crumbs. In 12-inch nonstick skillet, heat olive oil over medium-high heat and lightly brown chicken. Remove chicken and set aside.

2. In same skillet, stir in Ragú Cheese Creations! Sauce and bring to a boil. Reduce heat to low. Return chicken to skillet; arrange 1 tomato slice on each chicken breast half. Cover and simmer 5 minutes.

3. Evenly top chicken with cheese and simmer covered an additional 2 minutes or until chicken is thoroughly cooked. Serve, if desired, over hot cooked pasta and garnish with chopped fresh basil or parsley.

Makes 4 servings

Prep Time: 5 minutes
Cook Time: 25 minutes

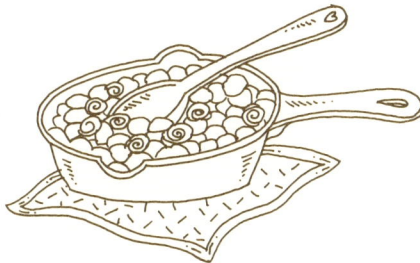

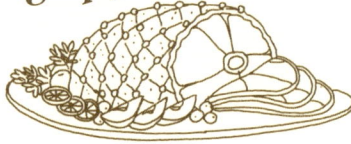

Supper-Time Favorites

Roasted Chicken & Vegetables

3 pounds chicken parts
1 cup LAWRY'S® Herb & Garlic Marinade with Lemon Juice, divided
12 small portabello mushrooms, cut into ½-inch slices
6 cups fresh vegetables, cut into 1-inch chunks (onions, zucchini, bell pepper, mushrooms, eggplant, etc.)
¼ cup olive oil
1 tablespoon LAWRY'S® Seasoned Salt

Preheat oven to 375°F. Spray broiler pan bottom with nonstick cooking spray; arrange chicken skin-side-down in pan. Pour ⅔ cup Herb & Garlic Marinade over chicken. Bake 30 minutes. Turn chicken over and brush with remaining ⅓ cup Marinade. In large resealable plastic bag, toss vegetables with oil and Seasoned Salt. Arrange vegetables in pan around chicken. Return pan to oven and bake until chicken is no longer pink and juices run clear when cut (175° to 185°F at thickest point), about 25 to 30 minutes.   *Makes 4 to 6 servings*

Meal Idea: Serve with hot cooked rice, pasta or potatoes.

Variations: *Also excellent in this recipe:* LAWRY'S® Mesquite Marinade with Lime Juice, Lemon Pepper Marinade with Lemon Juice or Mediterranean Marinade with Lemon Juice.

Prep Time: 10 minutes
Cook Time: 55 to 60 minutes

Maple-Glazed Ham

1 (7-pound) fully cooked bone-in ham
  Whole cloves
½ cup maple syrup
1 teaspoon dry mustard
2 teaspoons cider vinegar

1. Preheat oven to 350°F.

2. Cut skin off ham; trim off excess fat. Score top of ham in diamond design; stud with cloves. Place ham, fat side up, on rack in shallow roasting pan. Insert ovenproof meat thermometer into thickest part of ham, not touching bone.

3. Bake 1 hour 45 minutes to 2 hours (15 to 17 minutes per pound), or until thermometer registers 160°F. While ham is baking, mix together maple syrup, mustard and vinegar. Remove ham from oven 30 minutes before baking is complete. Spoon maple glaze over top and sides of ham; return to oven and continue baking.

4. Take ham out of oven. Let stand 10 minutes before transferring to serving platter. Slice with large carving knife. Garnish, if desired.

Makes 8 to 10 servings

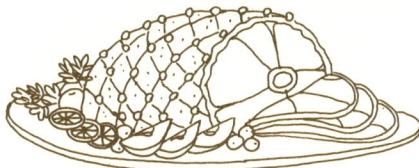

Salisbury Steak with Mushroom Sauce

1 pound 95% lean ground turkey or ground beef
3 tablespoons seasoned dry breadcrumbs
1 egg white
½ teaspoon salt
¼ teaspoon black pepper
   Butter-flavored nonstick cooking spray
½ cup chopped onion
2 packages (4 ounces each) sliced exotic mushrooms
   or 8 ounces sliced button mushrooms
½ teaspoon dried thyme leaves
1 tablespoon all-purpose flour
1 cup fat-free reduced-sodium beef broth
2 tablespoons chopped fresh thyme or parsley (optional)

1. Combine turkey, breadcrumbs, egg white, salt and pepper in medium bowl. Mix well; shape to form four ½-inch-thick patties.

2. Heat large nonstick skillet over medium heat; coat with cooking spray. Add patties; cook 5 minutes per side or until no longer pink in center. Remove from skillet; set aside.

3. Coat same skillet with cooking spray. Add onion; cook 3 minutes, stirring occasionally. Add mushrooms and dried thyme; cook 3 minutes. Sprinkle flour over vegetables; cook and stir 30 seconds. Add broth; bring to a boil. Reduce heat and simmer about 5 minutes until vegetables are tender and sauce has thickened. Return patties to skillet; heat through.

4. Serve patties with mushroom sauce and fresh thyme, if desired.

Makes 4 servings

Supper-Time Favorites

Perfect Crispy Catfish

2 tablespoons LAWRY'S® Perfect Blend Seasoning
    and Rub for Fish & Seafood
¾ cup yellow cornmeal
1 pound catfish fillets, cut into bite-size pieces
½ cup milk
¼ cup flour
⅓ cup vegetable oil

In large Ziploc® bag, combine Perfect Blend with cornmeal. Dip fish into milk; shake off excess milk. Add fish pieces to bag of seasoned cornmeal; shake to coat. Place flour in shallow pan then press coated fish into flour. Dip fish again in milk, then shake in bag of seasoned cornmeal again. In large electric fry pan, heat oil to 350°F; fry fish about 5 minutes on each side, depending upon thickness or until fish begins to flake easily.   *Makes 5 servings (about 8 pieces each)*

Hint: Coat fish ahead of time then place on tray, cover and refrigerate until ready to fry.

Prep Time: 20 minutes
Cook Time: 20 minutes

Ranch Chicken Nuggets

  WESSON® Vegetable Oil
2 cups self-rising flour
1 (1-ounce) package ranch dressing mix
2 cups buttermilk
1 (1-pound) frozen chicken tenders, cut into nuggets

Fill deep-fry pot to ½ its depth with Wesson Oil; heat to 350°F. In bowl, mix flour and dressing mix. Fill another bowl with buttermilk. Coat nuggets in flour mix, then buttermilk; return to flour mix. Fry 7 to 10 minutes or until golden brown; drain. Cool slightly.   *Makes 1 pound nuggets*

Prep Time: 10 minutes
Frying Time: 7 to 10 minutes

Supper-Time Favorites

Cheesy Ham & Broccoli Stuffed Potatoes

4 large baking potatoes
1 (5-ounce) can HORMEL® chunk ham, drained and flaked
½ package (10 ounces) frozen chopped broccoli, thawed and drained
1 cup sour cream with chive and onion seasoning
1 cup shredded Sharp Cheddar cheese, divided

Microwave potatoes on HIGH (100% power) 12 to 14 minutes or until fork tender. Wrap in foil and allow to stand 5 minutes. Slice away skin from top of each potato; carefully scoop out pulp, leaving shells intact. Mash pulp. Add chunk ham, broccoli, sour cream and ½ cup cheese to the potato pulp; stir well. Stuff shells with potato mixture; sprinkle with remaining cheese. Microwave on HIGH (100% power) 2 to 3 minutes or until cheese is melted.   *Makes 4 servings*

Steak with Mushroom Sauce

1½ pounds boneless beef sirloin steak
2 cups sliced fresh white mushrooms
1 medium onion, thinly sliced
1 (12-ounce) jar HEINZ® Fat Free Beef Gravy
1 tablespoon HEINZ® Tomato Ketchup
1 teaspoon HEINZ® Worcestershire Sauce
Dash pepper

Cut steak into 6 portions. Spray a large skillet with nonstick cooking spray. Cook steak over medium-high heat to desired doneness, about 5 minutes per side for medium rare. Remove and keep warm. In same skillet, cook mushrooms and onion until liquid evaporates. Stir in remaining ingredients; simmer 1 minute, stirring occasionally. Serve sauce over steak.   *Makes 6 servings*

Supper-Time Favorites

Meat Loaf

½ cup catsup
¼ cup brown sugar
2 teaspoons dry mustard
1 pound ground beef
½ cup bread crumbs
¼ cup MRS. DASH® Onion & Herb Blend
2 eggs
Vegetable cooking spray

Preheat oven to 350°F. Spray 8×4 inch loaf pan with vegetable cooking spray. Combine catsup, brown sugar and mustard in small bowl; mix well. Set aside. Combine ground beef, bread crumbs, Onion & Herb Blend, eggs and half of catsup sauce in large bowl; mix well. Pat into prepared loaf pan. Bake 40 minutes. Spread remaining catsup sauce over meat. Return to oven and cook additional 10 minutes. Let stand 5 minutes before serving. *Makes 6 servings*

Prep Time: 10 minutes
Cook Time: 55 minutes

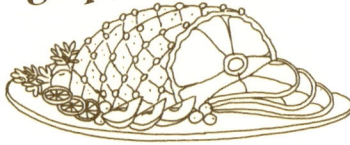

Supper-Time Favorites

Lemony Vegetable Salmon Pasta

½ pound salmon fillet
   Juice of 1 SUNKIST® lemon, divided
2 cups broccoli florets
2 medium carrots, thinly sliced diagonally
1 cup reduced-sodium chicken broth
1 teaspoon sesame oil
1 tablespoon cornstarch
1½ cups (4 ounces uncooked) spiral-shaped pasta, cooked and drained

In large non-stick skillet, cover salmon with water. Add juice of ½ lemon. Bring to a boil; reduce heat and simmer 10 to 12 minutes or until fish flakes easily with fork. Remove salmon; cool enough to remove skin and flake fish. Discard liquid. In clean skillet, combine broccoli, carrots, chicken broth and sesame oil. Bring to a boil. Reduce heat; cover and briskly simmer 5 minutes or until vegetables are just tender. Combine cornstarch with remaining juice of ½ lemon; stir into vegetable mixture. Cook, stirring, until mixture thickens. Add cooked pasta and reserved salmon; heat. Serve with lemon wedges, if desired. *Makes 4 servings*

Savory Crescent Turkey Squares

2 cups JENNIE-O TURKEY STORE® Fully Cooked Oven-Roasted
 Turkey Breast, cooked, cubed
1 package (3 ounces) cream cheese, softened
2 tablespoons butter or margarine, softened
2 tablespoons milk
1 tablespoon chopped onion
¼ teaspoon salt
¼ teaspoon black pepper
1 (8-ounce) tube refrigerated crescent roll dough
1 tablespoon butter or margarine, melted
½ cup seasoned croutons, crushed

Heat oven to 350°F. In bowl, combine cream cheese and 2 tablespoons softened butter. Stir until smooth. Add turkey, milk, onion, salt and black pepper. Separate dough into 4 rectangles, sealing perforations. Spoon ½ cup turkey mixture on one end of rectangle. Fold other end of dough over filling. Seal edges with fork. Place on baking pan. Brush tops with 1 tablespoon melted butter. Sprinkle with crushed croutons. Bake 20 to 25 minutes or until golden brown. *Makes 4 servings*

Cook Time: 30 minutes

Ground Beef Stroganoff

1 pound 95% lean ground beef
2 tablespoons MRS. DASH® Minced Onion Medley, divided
2 tablespoons butter
2 tablespoons flour
1 can (14½ ounces) beef broth
1 tablespoon tomato paste
1 can (7 ounces) sliced mushrooms, drained
1 cup sour cream
1 pound egg noodles, cooked
¼ cup finely chopped parsley

Cook ground beef and 1 tablespoon Mrs. Dash Minced Onion Medley in a medium skillet over medium heat for 4 to 5 minutes or until beef is browned and no longer pink. Remove from skillet. Melt butter in the same pan and whisk in flour and remaining 1 tablespoon Mrs. Dash Minced Onion Medley. Cook until slightly browned. Gradually whisk in broth and tomato paste. Cook for 2 to 3 minutes or until mixture thickens; whisk constantly. Stir in mushrooms and return beef to skillet. Heat until warmed. Remove from heat and stir in sour cream. Serve with noodles and top with parsley.

Makes 4 servings

Prep Time: 5 minutes
Cook Time: 10 minutes

Oven-Fried Asiago Chicken

1 tablespoon plus 1½ teaspoons Dijon mustard
1 tablespoon lemon juice
3 cloves garlic, minced
½ teaspoon dried rosemary
   Black pepper to taste
6 small chicken thighs, skinned
3 cups bran flakes cereal
6 tablespoons grated BELGIOIOSO® Asiago Cheese
   Lemon slices

Preheat oven to 350°F. In small bowl, combine mustard, lemon juice, garlic, rosemary and pepper. Coat chicken in mustard mixture.

In resealable plastic food storage bag, combine bran flakes and BelGioioso Asiago Cheese. Seal bag and crush flakes. Place chicken pieces in bag, a few at a time, and shake to coat with crumb mixture.

In baking dish coated with nonstick cooking spray, arrange chicken in single layer. Sprinkle remaining crumbs over top. Cover with foil and bake 20 minutes. Remove foil and bake 20 minutes longer or until juices run clear when pricked with fork. Garnish with lemon and serve.   *Makes 6 servings*

Cheesy Ham and Macaroni

    1 (1.8 ounce) package white sauce mix
    2 cups milk
    ½ cup grated Parmesan cheese
    ½ cup cubed American Cheese
    ⅛ teaspoon ground pepper
    7 ounces macaroni, cooked according to directions, drained
 1½ cups fully-cooked ham
    1 cup frozen green peas, thawed

In a large saucepan stir together white sauce mix and milk.* Following package directions, cook until thickened. Stir in cheeses and pepper. Add macaroni, ham and peas; cook, stirring until heated through. Serve hot.   *Makes 6 servings*

If you want to make a white sauce from scratch, melt 3 tablespoons butter in a saucepan. Stir in ¼ cup flour and cook until mixture bubbles. Stir in 2 cups milk and cook, stirring until thickened.

Favorite recipe from **National Pork Board**

Lemon-Garlic Chicken

    2 tablespoons olive oil
    2 cloves garlic, pressed
    1 teaspoon grated lemon peel
    1 teaspoon lemon juice
    ¼ teaspoon salt
    ¼ teaspoon black pepper
    4 skinless boneless chicken breast halves (about 1 pound)

Combine oil, garlic, lemon peel, lemon juice, salt and pepper in small bowl. Brush oil mixture over both sides of chicken to coat. Lightly oil grid to prevent sticking. Grill chicken over medium KINGSFORD® Briquets 8 to 10 minutes or until chicken is no longer pink in center, turning once.   *Makes 4 servings*

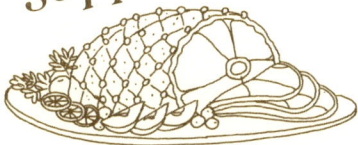

Harvest Pot Roast

1 large size (20×14-inch) oven cooking bag
¼ cup all-purpose flour
1 (2½- to 3-pound) ALWAYS TENDER® boneless pork roast
1 pound medium-size new red potatoes, quartered
1 large onion, cut into thin wedges
1 cup baby carrots, cut in half
2 stalks celery, cut diagonally into 1-inch pieces
1 cup vegetable juice
1 tablespoon HERB-OX® reduced sodium beef bouillon granules
1 clove garlic, minced
1 bay leaf

Preheat oven to 350°F. Add flour to oven bag; twist end of bag and shake to coat with flour. Place oven bag into a 13×9-inch baking dish. Add pork and remaining ingredients. Gently squeeze bag to blend ingredients. Close bag and secure with twist tie. Cut six (½-inch) slits in the top of the bag. Bake 2 to 2½ hours or until pork has reached an internal temperature of 160°F and the vegetables are fork tender.

Makes 6 servings

Prep Time: 15 minutes
Total Time: 2¾ hours

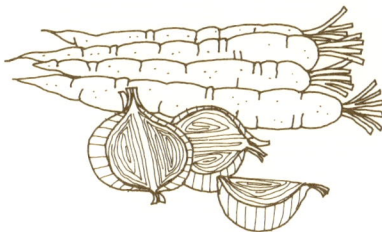

Supper-Time Favorites

Crusty Hot Pan-Fried Fish

1½ cups all-purpose flour
3½ teaspoons Chef Paul Prudhomme's Seafood Magic®
1 cup milk
1 large egg, beaten
6 fish fillets (4 ounces each), speckled trout or drum or your favorite fish
Vegetable oil for frying

In flat pan, combine flour and 2 teaspoons of the Seafood Magic®. In separate pan, combine milk and egg until well blended. Season fillets by sprinkling about ¼ teaspoon of the Seafood Magic® on each. In large skillet, heat about ¼ inch oil over medium heat until hot. Meanwhile, coat each fillet with seasoned flour, shake off excess and coat well with milk mixture; then, just before frying, coat fillets once more with flour, shaking off excess. Fry fillets in hot oil until golden brown, 1 to 2 minutes per side. Drain on paper towels and serve immediately on heated serving plates. *Makes 6 servings*

Original Ranch® Beef and Noodle Skillet

8 ounces uncooked wide egg noodles
1 pound lean ground beef, cooked and drained
1 container (8 ounces) sour cream (1 cup)
¾ cup milk
1 jar (4½ ounces) sliced mushrooms, drained
1 packet (1 ounce) HIDDEN VALLEY® The Original Ranch®
   Salad Dressing & Seasoning Mix
½ cup grated Parmesan cheese
Sliced green onions (optional)

Cook noodles according to package directions. Drain and combine with ground beef, sour cream, milk, mushrooms and salad dressing & seasoning mix. Cook and stir until thoroughly heated. Sprinkle with cheese. Garnish with onions, if desired. *Makes 4 servings*

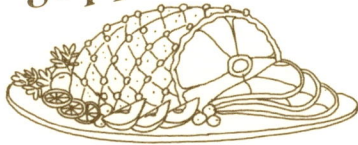

Lemon Chicken

2 tablespoons butter
1 tablespoon oil
4 chicken breasts, cut into strips
3 cups water
2 packages UNCLE BEN'S NATURAL SELECT® Garlic & Butter Flavor Rice
⅓ cup lemon juice
Pinch of rosemary
½ cup cream
¼ cup chopped parsley
1 cup spinach leaves
1 tomato (cut into pieces)

1. In a skillet, melt butter and oil over medium heat and sauté chicken until no pink remains.

2. Add the water, rice, lemon juice and rosemary and bring to a boil. Reduce heat; cover and simmer about 10 minutes.

3. Remove from heat; stir in cream and chopped parsley.

4. Serve over spinach leaves as bed and garnish with tomato for color.

Makes 6 servings

Prep Time: 10 minutes

Supper-Time Favorites

Shepherd's Pie

1 tablespoon vegetable oil
2 teaspoons bottled or fresh minced garlic
1 package JENNIE-O TURKEY STORE® Lean Ground Turkey
½ teaspoon dried basil
½ teaspoon dried thyme
½ teaspoon salt
½ teaspoon freshly ground black pepper
1 can (10½ ounces) *or* 1 jar (12 ounces) turkey gravy
½ cup frozen corn kernels
½ cup frozen tiny peas
2½ cups prepared mashed potatoes, homemade or frozen prepared
½ cup (2 ounces) shredded cheddar cheese

Heat oil in 10-inch oven-proof skillet over medium-high heat. (If skillet is not oven-proof, wrap handle in double thickness of aluminum foil.) Add garlic. Crumble turkey into skillet; sprinkle with herbs, salt and pepper. Cook 5 minutes or until no longer pink, stirring occasionally. Add gravy, corn and peas; simmer uncovered 5 minutes or until vegetables are defrosted and mixture is very hot. Spoon mashed potatoes around edges of mixture, leaving 3-inch opening in center. Sprinkle cheese over all. Transfer skillet to broiler and broil about 4 to 5 inches from heat source for 2 to 3 minutes or until cheese is melted and mixture is bubbly.

Makes 6 servings

Supper-Time Favorites

Beef Tips and Egg Noodles

2 packages (0.88 ounce each) LAWRY'S® Brown Gravy Mix
1 can (6 ounces) tomato paste
½ teaspoon LAWRY'S® Seasoned Salt
2 tablespoons vegetable or olive oil
1½ pounds boneless beef top sirloin or sirloin tip, cut into ½-inch cubes
¼ cup chopped green bell pepper
8 ounces wide egg noodles, cooked

In medium bowl, whisk together Brown Gravy Mix, 2 cups water, tomato paste and Seasoned Salt until smooth; set aside. In large skillet, heat oil over high heat. Add beef and and bell pepper; cook until beef is browned, about 5 minutes. Stir in gravy mixture. Bring to a boil; reduce heat to low. Cover and cook 8 minutes, stirring occasionally. Serve over hot egg noodles. *Makes 4 to 6 servings*

Meal Idea: Add 1 package (8 ounces) sliced fresh mushrooms or 1 can (4 ounces) sliced mushrooms; cook with gravy and peppers for extra flavor.

Hint: Sirloin is recommended since less tender cuts of beef need longer cooking times.

Prep Time: 10 to 12 minutes
Cook Time: 35 to 40 minutes

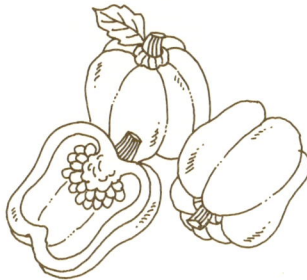

Dilly Salmon Cakes

1 can (14.75 ounces) pink salmon, skin and bones removed, flaked
1⅓ cups *French's*® French Fried Onions, divided
1 egg
¼ cup plus 2 tablespoons dry bread crumbs, divided
¼ cup chopped fresh parsley
2 tablespoons minced fresh dill *or* 2 teaspoons dried dill weed, divided
2 tablespoons low-fat mayonnaise
1 tablespoon lemon juice
Lettuce leaves
4 rolls
Tartar sauce

Combine salmon, ⅔ *cup* French Fried Onions, egg, ¼ cup bread crumbs, parsley, 1½ tablespoons (1½ teaspoons dried) dill, mayonnaise and lemon juice in large bowl; mix well. Shape into 4 oval patties, about ¾ inch thick. Pour remaining 2 tablespoons bread crumbs onto sheet of waxed paper. Coat salmon patties with bread crumbs.

Spray large nonstick skillet with nonstick cooking spray; heat over medium heat. Add patties; cook 8 minutes or until golden brown, turning halfway through cooking time. Transfer to serving platter.

Add remaining ⅔ *cup* onions and dill to skillet. Cook and stir 30 seconds or until golden.

Serve salmon cakes on lettuce-lined rolls. Top with tartar sauce and seasoned onions.

Makes 4 servings

Prep Time: 20 minutes
Cook Time: 10 minutes

Supper-Time Favorites

Turkey Pot Pie

  2 tablespoons butter or margarine
  1 cup chopped onion
  3 tablespoons all-purpose flour
1¼ teaspoons salt
  ¼ teaspoon freshly ground black pepper or ground white pepper
  1 package JENNIE-O TURKEY STORE® Breast Strips
  ¾ cup whipping cream or half-and-half
  1 package (10 ounces) frozen mixed vegetables, thawed,
      or 2 cups chopped cooked vegetables
  ¼ cup chopped parsley or chives (optional)
    Single pastry crust for 9- or 10-inch pie
  1 large egg, well-beaten

Heat oven to 400°F. Melt butter in large deep skillet over medium-high heat. Add onion; cook 5 minutes, stirring occasionally. Place flour, salt and pepper in plastic or paper bag. Add turkey; shake to coat. Add to skillet; cook 2 minutes, stirring occasionally. Add cream; mix well. Add vegetables; simmer uncovered 5 minutes (mixture will be very thick). Remove from heat; stir in parsley. Transfer mixture to 10-inch deep dish pie plate or quiche dish. Cut 4 slits in pastry to allow steam to escape. Place pastry over dish; seal edges. Brush egg lightly over pastry. Bake 25 to 30 minutes or until pastry is golden brown and mixture is bubbly. Let stand 5 minutes before serving. *Makes 6 servings*

Cook Time: 30 minutes

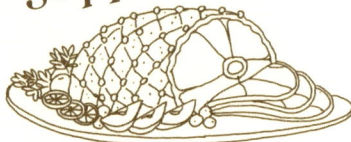

Supper-Time Favorites

Country-Style Pot Roast

1 (3- to 3½-pound) boneless beef pot roast (rump, chuck or round)
1 envelope LIPTON® RECIPE SECRETS® Onion Soup Mix*
2½ cups water, divided
4 medium all-purpose potatoes, cut into 1-inch pieces (about 2 pounds)
4 carrots, sliced
2 to 4 tablespoons all-purpose flour

Also terrific with LIPTON® RECIPE SECRETS® Onion Mushroom, Beefy Onion or Beefy Mushroom Soup Mix.

1. In Dutch oven or 6-quart saucepot, brown roast over medium-high heat. Add soup mix blended with 2 cups water. Bring to a boil over high heat. Reduce heat to low and simmer covered, turning roast occasionally, 2 hours.

2. Add vegetables and cook an additional 30 minutes or until vegetables and roast are tender; remove roast and vegetables.

3. For gravy, blend remaining ½ cup water with flour; add to Dutch oven. Bring to a boil over high heat. Reduce heat to low and simmer uncovered, stirring constantly, until thickened, about 5 minutes.   *Makes 8 servings*

Slow Cooker Method: In slow cooker, add vegetables, then roast. Add soup mix blended with 2 cups water. Cook covered on LOW 8 to 10 hours or HIGH 4 to 6 hours or until roast is tender. Remove roast and vegetables to serving platter. Blend remaining water with flour and stir into juices in slow cooker. Cook covered on HIGH 15 minutes or until thickened.

Prep Time: 10 minutes
Cook Time: 2 hours 40 minutes

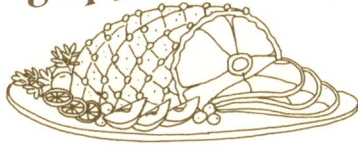 

Supper-Time Favorites

Creole Smothered Pork

Nonstick cooking spray
4 bone-in pork loin chops (5 ounces each), trimmed of fat
1 cup chopped green bell pepper
¾ cup chopped yellow onion
¾ cup thinly sliced celery
1 (14½-ounce) can stewed tomatoes
1 cup fresh or frozen cut okra, thawed
½ teaspoon dried thyme leaves
1 bay leaf
1 packet boil-in-a-bag rice *or* 1 cup uncooked instant rice
¼ cup chopped fresh parsley
¼ teaspoon salt
⅛ to ¼ teaspoon hot pepper sauce
2 teaspoons olive oil

1. Spray 12-inch nonstick skillet with cooking spray; heat over medium-high heat until hot. Add pork; cook 4 minutes or until lightly browned on one side. Remove pork from skillet; set aside, browned side up.

2. Add peppers, onions and celery to drippings in skillet; lightly spray with cooking spray. Cook and stir over medium-high heat 4 minutes or until onions are translucent. Add tomatoes, okra, thyme and bay leaf to skillet. Bring to a boil over medium-high heat. Add pork and any accumulated juices; spoon some sauce over all. Reduce heat. Cover tightly; simmer 10 minutes or until pork is no longer pink in center. Remove pork to serving platter; keep warm.

3. Meanwhile, cook rice according to package directions, omitting salt and fat.

4. Increase heat of skillet to medium-high. Bring tomato mixture to a boil; cook 1 minute to reduce slightly. Remove skillet from heat. Add parsley, salt and hot pepper sauce; stir to blend. Spoon rice around outer edges of pork chops. Spoon tomato mixture over pork. Drizzle with olive oil.   *Makes 4 servings*

Prep Time: 20 minutes
Cook Time: 11 minutes

Supper-Time Favorites

Garlic & Herb Chicken Sauté

1 pound boneless, skinless chicken,* cut into strips
1 cup KC MASTERPIECE™ Garlic & Herb Marinade, divided
1 tablespoon vegetable oil
6 cups assorted fresh vegetables,** such as broccoli florets, sliced
    mushrooms, sliced carrots, chopped onion and bell pepper
  Hot cooked rice

Strips of lean pork can be substituted for chicken.

**For a quick and easy version, substitute 6 cups assorted frozen vegetables; cook as directed above.*

Place chicken in bowl and add ½ cup Garlic & Herb Marinade; stir to coat. Marinate in refrigerator for 10 minutes. Heat oil in large nonstick skillet over high heat. Stir in vegetables and sauté until crisp-tender, about 7 minutes. Remove from skillet; set aside. Sauté marinated chicken in hot skillet until chicken is opaque, about 4 minutes. Add reserved vegetables and remaining ½ cup marinade to chicken; stir to combine. Heat thoroughly. Serve immediately with hot cooked rice.
Makes 4 servings

Sweet 'N' Tangy Glazed Chicken

⅓ cup *Frank's® RedHot®* Original Cayenne Pepper Sauce
⅓ cup *French's®* Bold n' Spicy Brown Mustard *or* Honey Dijon Mustard
⅓ cup honey
 3 pounds chicken parts

1. Preheat oven to 400°F. Combine *Frank's RedHot* Sauce, mustard and honey in a well-greased 3-quart baking dish.

2. Dip chicken pieces in mixture; arrange skin-side up in single layer. Bake 45 minutes or until chicken is no longer pink near bone, basting occasionally. Serve chicken with sauce from pan.
Makes 4 servings

Prep Time: 5 minutes
Cook Time: 45 minutes

Supper-Time Favorites

London City Broil
with Onion Marmalade

 2 pounds top round steak
½ cup balsamic vinegar or red wine vinegar
¼ cup olive oil
¼ cup *French's*® Bold n' Spicy Brown Mustard
 2 cloves garlic, pressed
½ teaspoon salt
½ teaspoon black pepper

Onion Marmalade
¼ cup butter or margarine
 4 medium red onions, thinly sliced
⅓ cup *French's*® Bold n' Spicy Brown Mustard
¼ cup balsamic vinegar or red wine vinegar
¾ teaspoon salt

1. Place steak in large resealable plastic food storage bag. Combine ½ cup vinegar, oil, ¼ cup mustard, garlic, ½ teaspoon salt and pepper in small bowl. Pour over steak; turn steak to coat evenly. Seal bag and marinate in refrigerator 1 hour.

2. To prepare Onion Marmalade, melt butter in large skillet over medium-high heat. Add onions; cook until very tender, stirring constantly. Add ⅓ cup mustard, ¼ cup vinegar and ¾ teaspoon salt. Cook over medium-low heat until mixture thickens, stirring often.

3. Place steak on grid, reserving marinade. Grill over high heat 15 minutes for medium rare or to desired doneness, turning and basting often with marinade. *Do not baste during last 5 minutes of cooking.* Slice steak diagonally into thin pieces and serve with Onion Marmalade. *Makes 8 servings*

Prep Time: 20 minutes
Marinate Time: 1 hour
Cook Time: 30 minutes

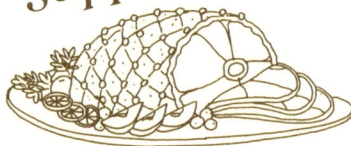

Supper-Time Favorites

Macaroni and Cheese Pronto

8 ounces uncooked elbow macaroni
1 can (10¾ ounces) cream of Cheddar soup
½ cup milk
2 cups diced cooked ham (about ½ pound)
1 cup (4 ounces) shredded Cheddar cheese
½ cup frozen green peas
Black pepper

1. Cook macaroni according to package directions. Drain and set aside.

2. While macaroni is cooking, combine soup and milk in medium saucepan. Cook and stir over medium heat until smooth.

3. Add ham, cheese, peas and cooked macaroni to soup mixture. Reduce heat to low; cook and stir 5 minutes or until cheese melts and mixture is heated through. Add pepper to taste. *Makes 4 servings*

Tip: For a special touch, garnish Macaroni and Cheese Pronto with fresh Italian parsley before serving.

Cook's Notes: Perfectly cooked pasta should be al dente—tender but still firm to the bite. Test pasta shortly before the time recommended on the package to avoid overcooking.

Prep and Cook Time: 20 minutes

Supper-Time Favorites

Pasta with Chicken and Peppers

5 tablespoons FILIPPO BERIO® Extra Virgin Olive Oil, divided
1 pound boneless chicken breasts, skinned and cut into julienne strips
1 medium onion, chopped
1 medium red bell pepper, cut into julienne strips
1 medium green bell pepper, cut into julienne strips
1 clove garlic, minced
⅛ teaspoon ground red pepper
2 large tomatoes, chopped
¾ pound uncooked tubular pasta, such as penne

1. Heat 2 tablespoons olive oil over medium heat in large skillet. Sauté chicken until it turns white. Remove chicken; set aside.

2. Add 2 tablespoons olive oil to skillet; cook and stir onion and bell peppers until tender.

3. Return chicken to pan; add garlic and ground red pepper. Cook for 3 minutes, stirring constantly.

4. Add tomatoes; simmer for 10 minutes.

5. While chicken mixture is simmering, cook pasta according to package directions; do not overcook. Drain and toss with remaining 1 tablespoon olive oil in large bowl. Serve with sauce.   *Makes 4 servings*

Prep Time: 15 minutes
Cook time: 25 minutes

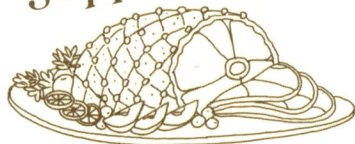

Supper-Time Favorites

Country Pork Skillet

4 boneless pork chops, diced
1 (12-ounce) jar pork gravy
2 tablespoons ketchup
8 small red potatoes, diced
2 cups frozen mixed vegetables

In large skillet, brown pork; stir in gravy, ketchup and potatoes. Cover; simmer for 10 minutes. Stir in vegetables; cook for 10 to 15 minutes longer until vegetables are tender.

Makes 4 servings

Favorite recipe from **National Pork Board**

Garlic-Pepper Steak

1¼ teaspoons LAWRY'S® Garlic Powder With Parsley
1 pound beef sirloin steak
1¼ teaspoons LAWRY'S® Seasoned Pepper
½ teaspoon LAWRY'S® Seasoned Salt

Press Garlic Powder With Parsley into both sides of steak with back of spoon. Sprinkle both sides with Seasoned Pepper and Seasoned Salt. Cover and refrigerate for 30 minutes; grill or broil for about 4 to 7 minutes per side or until desired doneness.

Makes 4 servings

Meal Idea: Serve with hot baked potatoes and a crisp green salad.

Prep Time: 3 to 4 minutes
Cook Time: 8 to 14 minutes

Supper-Time Favorites

Beef & Mushroom Stroganoff

1 pound boneless beef sirloin or top round steak, thinly sliced
½ teaspoon ground black pepper
2 tablespoons margarine or butter, divided
3 cups (8 ounces) sliced mushrooms
½ cup chopped onion
1 (14½-ounce) can beef broth
½ cup milk
1 (4.8-ounce) package PASTA RONI® Parmesano
¾ cup frozen peas
⅓ cup sour cream

1. Sprinkle steak with pepper. In large skillet over medium-high heat, melt 1 tablespoon margarine. Add steak strips; sauté 2 minutes or until no longer pink. Remove from skillet; set aside.

2. In same skillet over medium heat, melt remaining 1 tablespoon margarine. Add mushrooms and onion; sauté 6 minutes.

3. Add beef broth and milk; bring to a boil. Stir in pasta, steak, peas and Special Seasonings. Reduce heat to medium-low. Gently boil, uncovered, 4 to 6 minutes or until pasta is tender, stirring frequently. Stir in sour cream; let stand 5 minutes before serving.

Makes 4 servings

Prep Time: 10 minutes
Cook Time: 20 minutes

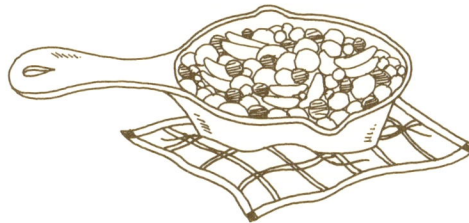

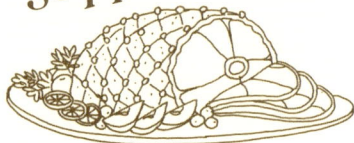

Supper-Time Favorites

Perfect Oven "Fried" Chicken

2 tablespoons LAWRY'S® Perfect Blend Seasoning
    and Rub for Chicken & Poultry
½ cup light mayonnaise
4 boneless, skinless chicken breasts
5 cups crushed corn flake cereal

Preheat oven to 400°F. In large Ziploc® bag, mix Perfect Blend with mayonnaise. Add chicken to bag and shake until completely coated. Place corn flakes in another large Ziploc® bag; seal and crush. Drop chicken, one piece at a time, into crushed flakes and shake to coat. Set cooling rack on foil-lined baking sheet; spray with nonstick cooking spray. Place chicken on rack and bake until no longer pink and juices run clear when cut, about 35 minutes.   *Makes 4 servings*

Prep Time: 10 minutes
Cook Time: 35 minutes

Western Skillet Noodles

½ pound ground beef
2 teaspoons chili powder
2⅓ cups water
1 can (11 ounces) whole kernel corn with sweet peppers, drained
1 tablespoon I CAN'T BELIEVE IT'S NOT BUTTER!® Spread
1 package LIPTON® Sides Noodles & Sauce—Beef Flavor
½ cup shredded cheddar cheese (about 2 ounces), divided

Brown ground beef with chili powder in 12-inch nonstick skillet over medium-high heat; drain. Remove and set aside.

Add water, corn and I Can't Believe It's Not Butter!® Spread and bring to a boil. Stir in Noodles & Sauce—Beef Flavor and continue boiling over medium heat, stirring occasionally, 7 minutes or until noodles are tender.

Stir in beef mixture and ¼ cup cheese; heat through. Top with remaining ¼ cup cheese.   *Makes about 2 servings*

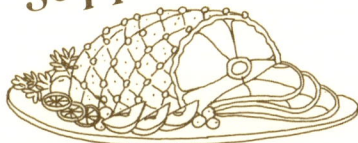

Pork Chops with Red Cabbage and Apples

1 teaspoon Chinese five-spice powder*
½ teaspoon salt substitute
½ teaspoon ground black pepper
3 center-cut pork loin chops (4 to 5 ounces each), trimmed of fat
2 teaspoons olive oil
1 large Granny Smith apple, cored and sliced
2 tablespoons chopped shallots
1 teaspoon margarine
½ head red cabbage, grated (about 4 cups)
1 teaspoon sucralose-based sugar substitute
½ teaspoon red wine vinegar
½ teaspoon lemon juice
   Additional salt substitute and pepper to taste
⅓ cup sugar-free applesauce (optional)

Chinese five-spice powder is a blend of cinnamon, cloves, fennel seed, anise and Szechuan pepper. It is available in most supermarkets and at Asian grocery stores.

1. Mix five-spice powder, salt substitute and pepper. Sprinkle mixture evenly over pork chops; set aside. Heat oil in large heavy nonstick skillet over medium heat. Place pork chops in skillet; brown both sides, turning after 2 minutes. Reduce heat to low. Cover; cook 15 to 20 minutes, turning chops several times until internal temperature of chops reaches 140°F.

2. Place apple, shallots and margarine in another large nonstick skillet. Cook and stir over medium heat 4 to 5 minutes. Add cabbage, sugar substitute, vinegar and lemon juice. Cook and stir until cabbage is wilted and tender. Season with salt substitute and black pepper.

3. Serve pork chop with 1 cup cabbage and apple mixture. Garnish, if desired, with 2 tablespoons sugar-free applesauce.   *Makes 3 servings*

Supper-Time Favorites

Corned Beef Dinner

1 corned beef brisket (about 5 pounds)
2 medium onions, peeled and quartered
4 peppercorns
1 bay leaf
½ teaspoon dried rosemary leaves
1 quart (4 cups) water
6 medium potatoes (about 2 pounds), peeled and quartered
6 medium carrots, peeled and cut into 2-inch pieces
2 ribs celery, cut into 2-inch pieces (about 1 cup)
1 medium head green cabbage, cut into wedges

Horseradish Sauce
2 tablespoons CRISCO® Stick or 2 tablespoons CRISCO® Shortening
2 tablespoons all-purpose flour
½ teaspoon salt
⅛ teaspoon black pepper
1 egg yolk
1 cup milk
2 teaspoons prepared horseradish, or to taste
1 tablespoon lemon juice

Put beef into a large Dutch oven with a tight-fitting cover. Add onions, peppercorns, bay leaf, rosemary and water. Bring to a boil and simmer covered for 3½ hours or until meat is fork tender. Add potatoes, carrots and celery to Dutch oven. Place cabbage on top of meat. Cover and cook for 1 hour or until tender. Remove vegetables and meat to a large platter. Serve with Horseradish Sauce.

For Horseradish Sauce, melt CRISCO® Shortening in a saucepan over medium heat. Stir in flour, salt and pepper. Mix well and cook until bubbly (about 1 minute). Remove from heat. Beat egg yolk; add milk and mix well. Stir into CRISCO® mixture. Cook over medium heat, stirring constantly for 3 minutes or until smooth and thickened. Remove from heat. Stir in horseradish and lemon juice.

Makes 12 servings

Rosemary Roasted Chicken and Potatoes

1 BUTTERBALL® Fresh Young Roaster, giblets removed
3 cloves garlic, minced
  Grated peel and juice of 1 lemon
2 tablespoons vegetable oil
1 tablespoon fresh rosemary leaves
1 teaspoon cracked black pepper
¼ teaspoon salt
6 medium potatoes, cut into pieces

Preheat oven to 425°F. Mix garlic, lemon peel, lemon juice, oil, rosemary, pepper and salt in medium bowl. Place chicken, breast side up, in lightly oiled large roasting pan. Place potatoes around chicken. Drizzle garlic mixture over chicken and onto potatoes. Bake 20 to 25 minutes per pound or until internal temperature reaches 180°F in thigh. Stir potatoes occasionally to brown evenly. Let chicken stand 10 minutes before carving. *Makes 8 servings*

Prep Time: 15 minutes plus roasting time

Savory Baked Fish

6 boneless fish fillets, such as scrod, flounder or other mild white fish
  (about 8 ounces each)
¾ cup HIDDEN VALLEY® The Original Ranch® Dressing
  Julienned vegetables, cooked (optional)

Arrange fish fillets in a large oiled baking pan. Spread each fillet with 2 tablespoons dressing. Bake at 375°F. for 10 to 20 minutes, depending on thickness of fish, or until fish flakes when tested with a fork. Finish under broiler to brown top. Serve on julienned vegetables, if desired. *Makes 6 servings*

Sauerbraten

3 large onions, sliced
8 tablespoons Butter Flavor CRISCO® Stick or 8 tablespoons Butter Flavor
    CRISCO® Shortening, divided
3 cups cider vinegar
1 cup packed dark brown sugar
20 whole cloves
10 peppercorns
6 bay leaves
10 gingersnap cookies, crushed
3 cups water, divided
1 (4- to 6-pound) beef rump roast
½ cup sour cream
½ cup golden raisins

Cook the sliced onions in 2 tablespoons CRISCO® Shortening until golden brown. Carefully add vinegar, brown sugar, cloves, peppercorns, bay leaves and cookies. Bring to a boil. Add 1 cup water; remove from heat and cool to room temperature.

Place rump roast and cooled marinade in smallest possible container. Cover with plastic wrap. Marinate in refrigerator for 3 days, turning meat 1 to 2 times per day. Remove roast from container; reserve marinade. Pat roast dry with paper towel.

Preheat oven to 350°F.

Melt 6 tablespoons CRISCO® Shortening in a large skillet and brown roast on all sides. Place in roasting pan and roast, uncovered, for approximately 2½ hours or until internal temperature reaches 165°F. Let meat rest 20 minutes before carving.

Meanwhile, bring marinade to a boil and reduce by half; strain. Stir in sour cream and golden raisins. Serve sauce with roast.   *Makes 6 to 8 servings*

Supper-Time Favorites

Savory Sauced Turkey with Noodles

1 package JENNIE-O TURKEY STORE® Turkey Breast Slices
2 tablespoons all-purpose flour
½ teaspoon each salt and dried, crushed thyme
¼ teaspoon each pepper and ground allspice
2 tablespoons margarine or butter, divided
½ cup chopped, trimmed green onions
2 small Golden Delicious apples, cored and thinly sliced
1 cup each low-fat milk and apple juice
1 tablespoon Dijon-style mustard
　Hot cooked spinach or egg noodles
　Green onions (optional)

Cut across grain of turkey slices to make strips ½ inch wide and 2½ inches long. In small bowl, combine flour, salt, thyme, pepper and allspice; set aside. In large skillet over medium heat, melt 1 tablespoon margarine. Cook and stir turkey until no longer pink, about 4 minutes. Remove from pan. Heat remaining 1 tablespoon margarine in skillet. Cook and stir onions and apples until tender, about 3 minutes. Sprinkle in flour mixture; cook for 1 minute. Stir in turkey, milk, apple juice and mustard. Bring to a boil and cook until thickened, about 2 minutes, stirring constantly. Serve over noodles. Garnish with green onions, if desired.

Makes 4 servings

Prep Time: 15 minutes
Cook Time: 30 minutes

Tuna Potpies

FILLING
- 2 tablespoons CRISCO® Oil*
- 3 medium carrots, thinly sliced
- 1 small onion, finely chopped
- 2 tablespoons all-purpose flour
- 1 can (12 ounces) evaporated skimmed milk
- 1 cup water
- 1 package (9 ounces) frozen cut green beans *or* peas
- 1 can (16 ounces) whole potatoes, drained and chopped
- 1 can (12½ to 13 ounces) solid white tuna in water, drained and flaked
- 1 tablespoon minced fresh dill *or* ¼ teaspoon dried dill weed
- ¼ teaspoon salt

CRUST
- 1¼ cups all-purpose flour
- 1 teaspoon baking powder
- ¼ cup cold water
- 3 tablespoons CRISCO® Oil

Use your favorite Crisco Oil product.

1. *For filling,* heat oil in large saucepan on medium heat. Add carrots and onion. Cook and stir until tender. Stir in flour. Cook one minute. Stir in milk and water gradually. Cook and stir until mixture thickens slightly.

2. Add beans, stirring to separate. Remove saucepan from heat. Stir in potatoes, tuna, dill and salt. Spoon into 4 (14 ounces *each*) ramekins.*

3. Heat oven to 400°F. Place cooling rack on countertop.

4. *For crust,* combine flour and baking powder in medium bowl.

5. Combine water and oil in small bowl. Add to flour mixture. Stir with fork until mixture forms large clumps. Press with fingers to form ball. Divide into 4 sections. Flatten between hands to form 4 "pancakes."

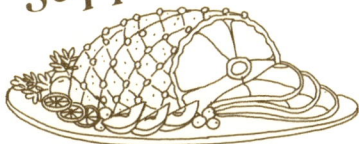
6. Roll each "pancake" between two sheets of waxed paper (or plastic wrap) on dampened countertop. Peel off top sheet.

7. Trim dough 1 inch larger than top of ramekin. Moisten outside edge of ramekin with water. Flip dough over onto ramekin. Fold edge under; flute. Cut decorative shapes or slits in dough for steam to escape. Place ramekins on baking sheet.

8. Bake at 400°F for 25 to 30 minutes or until filling is bubbly and crust is golden brown. *Do not overbake.* Remove sheet to cooling rack.   *Makes 4 servings*

*Substitute one 2-quart casserole for 4 ramekins. Roll dough to fit top of casserole. Bake at 400°F for 30 to 35 minutes.

Tortilla Crunch Chicken

1 envelope LIPTON® RECIPE SECRETS® Onion Soup Mix
1 cup finely crushed plain tortilla chips or cornflakes (about 3 ounces)
2½- to 3-pound chicken, cut into serving pieces (skinned, if desired) *or*
    6 boneless, skinless chicken breast halves (about 1½ pounds)
1 egg
2 tablespoons water
2 tablespoons melted margarine or butter

Preheat oven to 400°F.

In medium bowl, combine onion soup mix and tortilla chips. Dip chicken in egg beaten with water, then tortilla mixture, coating well. In 13×9-inch baking or roasting pan sprayed with no stick cooking spray, arrange chicken; drizzle with margarine.

For CHICKEN PIECES, bake uncovered 40 minutes or until chicken is thoroughly cooked.

For CHICKEN BREAST HALVES, bake uncovered 15 minutes or until chicken is thoroughly cooked.   *Makes about 4 servings*

Serving Suggestion: Serve chicken with your favorite fresh or prepared salsa.

Barbecued Meat Loaf

1 envelope LIPTON® RECIPE SECRETS® Onion Soup Mix
2 pounds ground beef
1½ cups fresh bread crumbs
2 eggs
¾ cup water
⅔ cup barbecue sauce

1. Preheat oven to 350°F. In large bowl, combine all ingredients except ⅓ cup barbecue sauce.

2. In 13×9-inch baking or roasting pan, shape beef mixture into loaf. Top with reserved barbecue sauce.

3. Bake uncovered 1 hour or until done. Let stand 10 minutes before serving.
Makes 8 servings

Home-Style Beef Brisket

1 envelope LIPTON® RECIPE SECRETS® Onion Soup Mix*
¾ cup water
½ cup ketchup
1 teaspoon garlic powder
½ teaspoon ground black pepper
1 (3-pound) boneless brisket of beef

Also terrific with LIPTON® RECIPE SECRETS® Onion Mushroom, Beefy Mushroom, Beefy Onion, Savory Herb with Garlic or Fiesta Herb with Red Pepper Soup Mix.

1. Preheat oven to 325°F. In 13×9-inch baking or roasting pan, add soup mix blended with water, ketchup, garlic powder and pepper.

2. Add brisket; turn to coat. Loosely cover with aluminum foil and bake 3 hours or until brisket is tender. If desired, thicken gravy. *Makes 8 servings*

Tip: For a quick one-dish dinner, during last hour of baking add ½ pound carrots, and 1 pound potatoes, cut into 2-inch chunks.

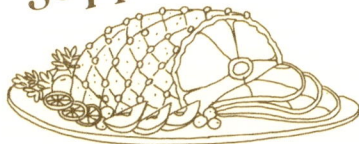

Supper-Time Favorites

Bistro Steak with Mushrooms

1½ to 2 pounds boneless sirloin steak (1½ inches thick)
2 cups sliced mushrooms
1 can (10¾ ounces) condensed golden mushroom soup
½ cup dry red wine or beef broth
3 tablespoons *French's*® Worcestershire Sauce

1. Rub sides of steak with *¼ teaspoon pepper*. Heat *1 tablespoon oil* over medium-high heat in nonstick skillet. Cook steak about 5 minutes per side for medium-rare or to desired doneness. Transfer steak to platter.

2. Stir-fry mushrooms in same skillet in *1 tablespoon oil* until browned. Stir in soup, wine, Worcestershire and *¼ cup water*. Bring to a boil. Simmer, stirring, 3 minutes. Return steak and juices to skillet. Cook until heated through. Serve with mashed potatoes, if desired. *Makes 6 servings*

Grilled Flank Steak

½ cup soy sauce
3 tablespoons packed brown sugar
3 tablespoons lime juice
2 tablespoons dry sherry (optional)
1 tablespoon grated fresh ginger *or* 1 teaspoon ground ginger
3 cloves garlic, minced
1 beef flank steak (1½ to 2 pounds)

Stir together soy sauce, sugar, lime juice, sherry, if desired, ginger and garlic until sugar is dissolved. Reserve ¼ cup marinade for basting. Place beef in large resealable plastic food storage bag; add remaining marinade. Seal bag; turn to coat evenly. Marinate in refrigerator several hours or overnight. Remove beef from marinade; discard marinade. Grill beef on covered grill over medium-hot KINGSFORD® Briquets 12 to 14 minutes until medium-rare or to desired doneness, turning once and basting with reserved ¼ cup marinade. Slice steak diagonally across grain into thin slices. *Makes 6 to 8 servings*

Cheesy Skillet Lasagna

1 pound ground beef
2 jars (14 ounces each) marinara sauce
2 cups cooked rotini pasta
1⅓ cups *French's*® French Fried Onions, divided
1 cup ricotta cheese
1 cup (4 ounces) shredded mozzarella cheese

1. Cook beef in large skillet until browned; drain. Stir in sauce, pasta and ⅔ *cup* French Fried Onions. Heat to boiling, stirring occasionally.

2. Spoon ricotta cheese over beef mixture. Sprinkle with mozzarella cheese and remaining ⅔ *cup* onions. Cover; cook over medium-low heat 3 minutes or until cheese melts.

Makes 4 servings

Prep Time: 10 minutes
Cook Time: 10 minutes

Prime Rib of Beef a la Lawry's®

1 (8 pound) prime rib roast
3½ tablespoons LAWRY'S® Seasoned Salt

Score fat on meat and rub generously with Seasoned Salt. Place prime rib on roasting rack in large roasting pan. Cook prime rib, uncovered, in preheated 325°F oven for 25 to 28 minutes per pound for medium rare or accelerate the cook time by cooking at 350°F for 18 to 22 minutes per pound. Remove roast from oven when internal temperature of roast reaches 125°F. Let stand 20 minutes before carving (internal temperature should rise to between 140 to 145°F).

Makes 8 servings

Prep Time: 5 minutes
Cook Time: varies with roast size (8-pound roast cooked rare to medium-rare takes 3 hours 20 minutes)

Supper-Time Favorites

Swedish Meatballs

  1 egg, beaten
2¼ cups milk or half-and-half, divided
  ¾ cup soft breadcrumbs
  ½ cup finely chopped onion
  ¼ cup snipped fresh parsley
  4 teaspoons HERB-OX® beef bouillon granules, divided
  ¼ teaspoon ground black pepper, divided
  ⅛ teaspoon ground allspice
  ½ pound lean ground beef
  ½ pound ground pork
  ¼ cup butter or margarine, divided
  2 tablespoons all-purpose flour
  3 cups hot cooked egg noodles

In bowl, combine egg and ¼ cup milk. Stir in breadcrumbs, onion, parsley,
2 teaspoons bouillon, ⅛ teaspoon pepper and allspice. Add meat and combine.
Shape mixture into 30 meatballs. In large skillet, heat 1 tablespoon butter. Place
half of the meatballs in skillet. Cook for 10 minutes or until no pink remains,
turning often to brown evenly. Repeat with remaining meatballs; set aside.
Add remaining 2 tablespoons butter to skillet and melt. Stir in flour, remaining
2 teaspoons bouillon and pepper. Gradually add remaining 2 cups milk or half-and-
half. Cook and stir over medium heat until thick and bubbly. Cook for 2 minutes.
Add meatballs to sauce. Serve over noodles.   *Makes 4 servings*

Prep Time: 30 minutes
Total Time: 1 hour

Side Dish Classics

Fried Green Tomatoes

½ pound sliced bacon
1 cup cornmeal
1 cup all-purpose flour
2 teaspoons salt
½ teaspoon black pepper
½ teaspoon cayenne pepper
3 eggs, slightly beaten
2 cups WESSON® Corn Oil
6 to 8 green tomatoes, sliced ¼ to ½ inch thick

In a large skillet, fry bacon until crisp; drain on paper towels. Crumble bacon; set aside. Reserve bacon drippings in the skillet. In a medium bowl, combine cornmeal, flour, salt and peppers; mix well. In a small bowl, combine eggs and *half* the crumbled bacon; mix well. Heat Wesson® Oil over medium heat in same skillet with bacon drippings. Sprinkle tomatoes lightly with salt; dip in egg mixture, making sure to press bacon pieces onto tomatoes. Place tomatoes in cornmeal mixture; gently press mixture onto both sides of tomatoes. Fry until light golden brown, turning once. Drain on paper towels. Sprinkle with *remaining* bacon and serve.   *Makes 20 to 25 fried tomatoes*

American Potato Salad

1½ pounds DOLE® Red or Yukon Gold Potatoes with skin on,
    cut into 1-inch cubes
1¼ teaspoons salt, divided
½ cup diced DOLE® Celery
¼ cup sliced DOLE® Green Onions
½ cup lowfat or regular mayonnaise
1 tablespoon white wine vinegar
2 teaspoons Dijon style mustard
⅛ teaspoon black pepper

• Cook potatoes in cold water to cover with 1 teaspoon salt in large pot. Bring to boil; lower heat and simmer 10 to 15 minutes or until tender. Drain and cool.

• Combine potatoes, celery and green onions in large bowl.

• Combine mayonnaise, vinegar, mustard, pepper and remaining ¼ teaspoon salt in small bowl. Pour dressing over potato mixture. Toss to evenly coat.

• Cover; refrigerate 1 hour to blend flavors.   *Makes 6 servings*

Prep Time: 15 minutes
Cook Time: 15 minutes

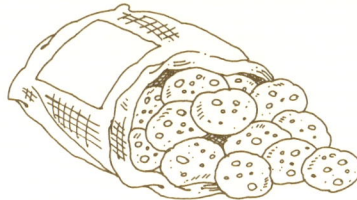

Side Dish Classics

Creamed Corn

1 package (22 ounces) frozen whole kernel corn, defrosted and drained
1 cup heavy cream
1 cup milk
½ teaspoon LAWRY'S® Seasoned Salt
3 tablespoons sugar
   Dash white pepper
⅓ cup butter, melted
½ cup flour

In large saucepan, combine corn, cream, milk, Seasoned Salt, sugar and white pepper; mix thoroughly. Heat over medium just until warm. In small bowl, whisk together butter and flour. Slowly add to corn mixture, stirring constantly. Bring just to a boil; quickly reduce heat to low and cook for 7 to 10 minutes, until slightly thickened. *Makes 4 to 6 servings*

Meal Idea: Serve with beef prime rib and a crisp green salad.

Prep Time: 3 minutes
Cook Time: 10 to 15 minutes

Side Dish   Classics

Apricot-Pineapple Mold

½ cup SMUCKER'S® Apricot Preserves
½ cup SMUCKER'S® Pineapple Topping
2 tablespoons vinegar
2½ cups water
1 teaspoon whole cloves
1 (4-inch) stick cinnamon
2 (3-ounce) packages orange-flavor gelatin
½ cup sour cream

In saucepan, combine preserves, pineapple topping, vinegar and water. Tie cloves and cinnamon in small square of cheesecloth and place in saucepan. Simmer mixture over low heat for 10 minutes. Remove spice bag.

Dissolve 1 package of gelatin in 2 cups of preserve mixture; stir until dissolved. Pour into 6-cup mold and refrigerate until almost firm.

Meanwhile, dissolve remaining package of gelatin in remaining preserve mixture; stir until dissolved. Refrigerate until partially set. Beat with electric mixer until fluffy. Fold in sour cream. Pour over first layer in mold. Refrigerate until firm, about 8 hours or overnight. Unmold to serve.   *Makes 8 to 10 servings*

Side Dish Classics

Scalloped Apples & Onions

1 medium onion, thinly sliced
4 tablespoons butter, melted, divided
5 red or green apples, cored and thinly sliced
8 ounces (1½ cups) pasteurized process cheese,
    cut into small pieces, divided
2 cups *French's*® French Fried Onions, divided

1. Preheat oven to 375°F. Sauté onion in 2 tablespoons butter in medium skillet over medium-high heat 3 minutes or until tender. Add apples and sauté 5 minutes or until apples are tender.

2. Stir 1 cup cheese, *1 cup* French Fried Onions and remaining 2 tablespoons melted butter into apple mixture. Transfer to greased 9-inch deep-dish pie plate.

3. Bake, uncovered, 20 minutes or until heated through. Top with remaining ½ cup cheese and 1 cup onions. Bake 5 minutes or until cheese is melted.

Makes 6 side-dish servings

Tip: To save time and cleanup, apple mixture may be baked in a heatproof skillet if desired. Wrap skillet handle in heavy-duty foil.

Variation: For added Cheddar flavor, substitute *French's*® **Cheddar French Fried Onions** for the original flavor.

Prep Time: 15 minutes
Cook Time: about 30 minutes

Side Dish Classics

Pineapple Lime Mold

1 can (20 ounces) DOLE® Pineapple Chunks
2 packages (3 ounces each) lime gelatin
2 cups boiling water
1 cup sour cream
½ cup chopped walnuts
½ cup chopped DOLE® Celery

Drain pineapple chunks, reserve syrup. Dissolve gelatin in boiling water. Add sour cream and reserved syrup. Chill until slightly thickened. Stir in pineapple chunks, walnuts and celery. Pour into 7-cup mold. Chill until set. *Makes 8 servings*

Baked Apple & Sweet Potato Casserole

6 sweet potatoes
3 Michigan Apples
2 tablespoons melted butter, divided
½ cup orange juice
¼ cup rum
¼ cup packed dark brown sugar
⅛ teaspoon ground cinnamon
⅛ teaspoon ground allspice

Preheat oven to 350°F. Boil or steam potatoes until tender. Remove skin and cut lengthwise into slices. Peel and core Michigan Apples; slice into rings. Grease 9×6-inch baking dish with 1 tablespoon butter. Layer potatoes and apples in dish. Combine orange juice, rum, brown sugar, cinnamon and allspice in medium bowl. Pour juice mixture over potato-apple layers. Drizzle with remaining 1 tablespoon butter. Bake 30 minutes or until brown, glazed and liquid is absorbed.

Makes 6 servings

Favorite recipe from **Michigan Apple Committee**

Side Dish Classics

Easy Cole Slaw

2 tablespoons CRISCO® Oil*
¼ cup granulated sugar
¼ cup cider vinegar
1 tablespoon prepared mustard
½ teaspoon salt
¼ teaspoon freshly ground black pepper
1 bag (1 pound) cole slaw mix (or shredded cabbage)

Use your favorite Crisco Oil product.

1. Combine oil, sugar, vinegar, mustard, salt and pepper in small saucepan. Place pan on medium heat. Simmer for 3 minutes.

2. Place cole slaw mix in mixing bowl. Toss with hot dressing. Let stand for 20 minutes. Serve with slotted spoon. *Makes 4 servings*

Note: This cole slaw can also be made up to 2 days in advance and refrigerated, tightly covered. Drain before serving.

Prep Time: 10 minutes
Total Time: 30 minutes

Side Dish Classics

Top of the Range Baked Beans

3 tablespoons CRISCO® Canola Oil
½ cup chopped onion
½ cup chopped green pepper
2 cans (16 ounces each) pork and beans
¾ cup catsup
¼ cup dark molasses
¼ cup packed light brown sugar
2 teaspoons prepared mustard

Variation
1 can (20 ounces) pineapple chunks, drained and chunks cut in half

Heat CRISCO® Canola Oil in a large saucepan or Dutch oven. Add onion and green pepper. Sauté for 5 minutes or until tender.

Stir in pork and beans, catsup, molasses, brown sugar, and mustard. Cover and cook over low heat for 20 minutes, or until mixture comes just to boiling, stirring frequently. Serve hot.   *Makes 10 to 12 servings*

Substitution: Substitute canned vegetarian baked beans for canned pork and beans to make this a vegetarian dish.

Variation: For an old classic flavored baked bean dish, add pineapple chunks to the pork and beans.

Vegetable Sunburst

3 medium carrots, thinly sliced (about 3 cups)
3 small zucchini, thinly sliced (about 3 cups)
1 cup (4 ounces) shredded Cheddar cheese
1⅓ cups *French's*® French Fried Onions, divided
1 can (10¾ ounces) condensed cream of celery soup
¼ cup milk
½ teaspoon seasoned salt
¼ teaspoon garlic powder
¼ teaspoon dried oregano leaves, crumbled

Preheat oven to 350°F. In medium saucepan, cook carrots in boiling water to cover just until tender-crisp. Place hot carrots under cold running water until cool enough to handle; drain. In 1½-quart casserole, arrange half the carrots around edge of dish; place half the zucchini in center. Sprinkle ½ cup cheese and ⅔ *cup* French Fried Onions over vegetables. In small bowl, combine soup, milk and seasonings. Pour half the soup mixture over onions. Arrange remaining zucchini around edge of casserole and remaining carrots in center. Pour remaining soup mixture over vegetables. Bake, covered, at 350°F for 30 minutes or until vegetables are tender. Top with remaining cheese and ⅔ *cup* onions; bake, uncovered, 5 minutes or until onions are golden brown.   *Makes 4 to 6 servings*

Microwave Directions: Place carrots and ½ cup water in medium microwave-safe bowl; cook on HIGH 5 to 7 minutes or until carrots are tender-crisp. Stir carrots halfway through cooking time. Drain. Prepare soup mixture as above. In 1½-quart microwave-safe casserole, layer vegetables, cheese, onions and soup mixture as above. Cook, covered, 8 to 10 minutes or until vegetables are tender. Rotate dish halfway through cooking time. Top with remaining cheese and onions; cook, uncovered, 1 minute or until cheese melts. Let stand 5 minutes.

Side Dish Classics

Cheddary Mashed Potato Bake

1 box (7.2 ounces) roasted garlic mashed potato mix
1 cup sour cream
1½ cups shredded Cheddar cheese, divided
1½ cups *French's*® **Cheddar French Fried Onions**

PREHEAT oven to 375°F. Make potatoes as directed on package for 2 pouches (8 servings). Stir in sour cream and 1 cup cheese. Heat through.

SPOON mixture into 2-quart baking dish. Sprinkle with remaining ½ cup cheese and French Fried Onions. Bake 10 minutes until hot and golden.

Makes 8 servings

Prep Time: 5 minutes
Cook Time: 10 minutes

Sweet and Sour Red Cabbage

1 small head red cabbage (1 pound), shredded
1 medium apple, unpeeled, cored, shredded
1 small potato, peeled, shredded
1 small onion, chopped
  Grated peel of ½ SUNKIST® lemon
  Juice of 1 SUNKIST® lemon
3 tablespoons firmly packed brown sugar
1 tablespoon red wine vinegar

In large, covered nonstick skillet, cook cabbage, apple, potato and onion in 1 cup water over low heat for 15 minutes; stir occasionally. Add lemon peel, lemon juice, brown sugar and vinegar. Cover; cook over low heat an additional 10 minutes, stirring often, until vegetables are tender and mixture thickens slightly.

Makes 6 servings

Side Dish Classics

Spiced Honey Carrots

    1 package (16 ounces) peeled baby carrots
1¼ cups boiling water
  ⅛ teaspoon ground cloves
  ⅛ teaspoon ground cinnamon
1½ tablespoons honey
    1 tablespoon 50% less fat margarine
     Grated peel and juice of ½ SUNKIST® lemon

In covered saucepan, cook carrots in gently boiling water with cloves and cinnamon until just tender, about 8 to 10 minutes; drain well. Add honey, margarine, lemon peel and lemon juice; heat through.

Makes 4 (⅔-cup) servings

Creamed Spinach

    2 cups milk
    1 package KNORR® Recipe Classics™ Leek Soup, Dip and Recipe Mix
    1 bag (16 ounces) frozen chopped spinach
  ⅛ teaspoon ground nutmeg

• In medium saucepan, combine milk and recipe mix. Bring to a boil over medium heat.

• Add spinach and nutmeg; stirring frequently. Bring to a boil over high heat. Reduce heat to low and simmer, stirring frequently, 5 minutes.

Makes 6 servings

Prep Time: 5 minutes
Cook Time: 10 minutes

Marinated Beet Salad

2 cans (15 ounces each) small, whole or sliced beets, undrained
½ cup white vinegar
¾ to 1 cup EQUAL® SPOONFUL*

*May substitute 18 to 24 packets EQUAL® sweetener.

- Combine beets, beet juice, vinegar and Equal® in medium bowl; cover tightly.

- Chill at least 8 hours before serving. Drain before serving.   *Makes 8 servings*

Homestead Succotash

¼ pound bacon, diced
1 cup chopped onion
½ teaspoon dried thyme leaves
1 can (15¼ ounces) DEL MONTE® Whole Kernel Golden Sweet Corn, drained
1 can (15¼ ounces) DEL MONTE Green Lima Beans, drained

1. Cook bacon in skillet until crisp; drain. Add onion and thyme; cook until onion is tender.

2. Stir in vegetables and heat through.   *Makes 6 to 8 servings*

Microwave Directions: In shallow 1-quart microwavable dish, cook bacon on HIGH 6 minutes or until crisp; drain. Add onion and thyme; cover and cook on HIGH 2 to 3 minutes or until onion is tender. Add vegetables. Cover and cook on HIGH 3 to 4 minutes or until heated through.

Prep & Cook Time for Stove Top: 13 minutes

Glazed Sweet Potatoes

1 cup frozen apple juice concentrate, thawed
⅓ cup EQUAL® SPOONFUL*
2 teaspoons cornstarch
1 teaspoon stick butter or margarine
1 teaspoon maple extract
1 teaspoon vanilla
2 pounds sweet potatoes, peeled, cut into 1-inch slices, cooked, kept warm

May substitute 8 packets EQUAL® sweetener.

● Heat apple juice concentrate, Equal® and cornstarch to boiling in small saucepan; boil, stirring constantly, until thickened. Remove from heat; stir in butter, maple extract and vanilla.

● Pour glaze over potatoes in serving bowl and toss gently.   *Makes 8 servings*

Succotash

1 tablespoon CRISCO® Pure Canola Oil
½ cup chopped red bell pepper
4 to 6 chopped scallions, white and green parts, separated
1 (10 ounce) package frozen baby lima beans, defrosted
1 (10 ounce) package frozen corn kernels, defrosted
¼ cup water
1 teaspoon salt
   Black pepper to taste

Heat the CRISCO® Pure Canola Oil in a large skillet or saucepan over medium heat. Add the red pepper and cook until just tender. Add the white parts of the scallions and stir. Add the lima beans, corn, water, salt and pepper, and stir well to combine.

Cover and cook about 5 minutes until the vegetables are cooked to your liking. Stir in the green parts of the scallions. Taste and add salt and pepper if needed.

Makes 4 to 6 servings

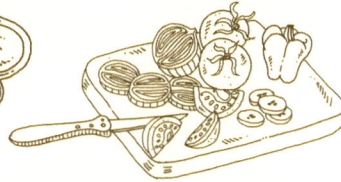

Side Dish Classics

Honey-Glazed Vegetable Medley

    1 cup peeled and thinly sliced carrots
    2 tablespoons water
    ¾ cup thinly sliced zucchini
    ¼ cup diced red bell pepper
    ¼ cup honey
    1 tablespoon butter or margarine
    1 tablespoon lemon juice
    ½ teaspoon salt
    ½ teaspoon ground ginger
    ½ teaspoon dried dill weed

Microwave Directions

Combine carrots and water in 1-quart microwave-safe dish. Cover and microwave at HIGH (100%) 3 to 4 minutes or until carrots are crisp-tender, stirring halfway through cooking time. Drain liquid; add remaining ingredients and mix thoroughly. Microwave at HIGH 2 to 2½ minutes or until zucchini is crisp-tender, stirring halfway through cooking time. Let stand 2 minutes and stir before serving.

Makes 2 servings

Favorite recipe from **National Honey Board**

Side Dish Classics

Orange Delight

2 packages (4-serving size) orange-flavored gelatin
2 cups hot water
2 cups cottage cheese
1 cup orange juice
1 cup pineapple juice
1 cup pecans
1 can (20 ounces) crushed pineapple, well-drained
6 tablespoons sugar
½ cup mayonnaise
1 pint whipping cream, whipped to stiff peaks

1. Dissolve gelatin in hot water in large serving bowl. Set aside.

2. Meanwhile, place cottage cheese in strainer and rinse under cold running water; drain thoroughly.

3. When gelatin has cooled and thickened, stir in cottage cheese and all remaining ingredients, except whipped cream. Stir to combine. Refrigerate until cool but not set; fold in whipped cream. Refrigerate 1 hour or until ready to serve.

Makes 8 to 10 servings

Magic Broiled Tomatoes

2 medium sized tomatoes, peeled
1 tablespoon plus 1 teaspoon unsalted butter, softened
2 teaspoons Chef Paul Prudhomme's Vegetable Magic®
1 tablespoon grated Parmesan cheese (optional)

Preheat the broiler. Score the tomatoes about 4 times across the top to about half-way down; set aside. Make a paste of the butter, the Vegetable Magic and the Parmesan, if desired. Spread half the mixture on top of each tomato pushing a little mixture down into the scoring. Place the tomatoes in a shallow pan, seasoned side up. Broil with tomato tops about 1 inch from heat until tops are brown and crusty, about 3 minutes. Serve immediately with any juices from the bottom of the pan spooned over the top.   *Makes 2 servings*

Savory Beets

2 tablespoons chopped onion
1 tablespoon butter or margarine
3 tablespoons honey
2 tablespoons wine vinegar
   Salt to taste
⅛ teaspoon ground cloves
1 can (16 ounces) sliced beets, drained

Sauté onion in butter in large skillet over medium heat until softened. Add honey, vinegar, salt and cloves; cook and stir until mixture begins to boil. Add beets; cook until thoroughly heated.   *Makes 4 servings*

Favorite recipe from **National Honey Board**

Glazed Brussels Sprouts and Pearl Onions

2 cups fresh brussels sprouts, trimmed
1 (10-ounce) package frozen pearl onions
3 tablespoons FLEISCHMANN'S® Original Margarine
1 pinch sugar
    Salt and freshly ground black pepper, to taste

1. Cook brussels sprouts in boiling salted water in large saucepan for 8 minutes. Add onions; cook for 4 minutes. Drain.

2. Melt margarine in large skillet over medium-high heat.

3. Add brussels sprouts mixture and sugar; cook and stir until onions are golden. Season with salt and pepper to taste.   *Makes 4 servings*

Prep Time: 5 minutes
Cook Time: 20 minutes
Total Time: 25 minutes

Side Dish Classics

Creamy Broccoli and Cheese

1 package (8 ounces) cream cheese, softened
¾ cup milk
1 packet (1 ounce) HIDDEN VALLEY® The Original Ranch®
    Salad Dressing & Seasoning Mix
1 pound fresh broccoli, cooked and drained
½ cup (2 ounces) shredded sharp Cheddar cheese

In a food processor fitted with a metal blade, blend cream cheese, milk and salad dressing & seasoning mix until smooth. Pour over broccoli in a 9-inch baking dish; stir well. Top with cheese. Bake at 350°F for 25 minutes or until cheese is melted.

Makes 4 servings

Blueberry-Peach Salad

1 package (6 ounces) orange-flavored gelatin
⅓ cup sugar
1 teaspoon finely shredded orange peel
2¼ cups orange juice, divided
2 cups buttermilk
1 can (8 ounces) crushed pineapple, drained
1 cup chopped pitted halved peeled peaches
1 cup fresh or frozen unsweetened blueberries, thawed
1 carton (8 ounces) dairy sour cream

In medium saucepan combine gelatin and sugar; stir in orange peel and 2 cups orange juice. Cook and stir until gelatin is dissolved; cool. Stir in buttermilk. Refrigerate until partially set. Fold in fruit; spoon into 10 individual molds. Refrigerate 6 hours or until firm. Combine sour cream and remaining ¼ cup orange juice; refrigerate. Unmold salad; serve with sour cream mixture.

Makes 10 servings

Favorite recipe from **Wisconsin Milk Marketing Board**

Side Dish   Classics

Double Cheddar Scalloped Potatoes

1 package (5 ounces) scalloped potato mix
2 cups boiling water
1 cup (4 ounces) shredded Cheddar cheese
¾ cup milk
¼ cup cooked crumbled bacon
1⅓ cups *French's*® French Fried Onions, divided
   Garnish: chopped parsley (optional)

1. Preheat oven to 400°F. Stir potatoes, sauce mix and boiling water in ungreased 1-quart casserole. Add cheese, milk, bacon and *⅔ cup* French Fried Onions; stir until well blended.

2. Bake, uncovered, 35 minutes or until top is golden and potatoes are tender.

3. Top with remaining onions. Let stand a few minutes for sauce to thicken. Garnish with parsley, if desired.   *Makes 6 servings*

Prep Time: 10 minutes
Cook Time: 35 minutes

Side Dish Classics

SPAM™ Cheesy Broccoli Bake

    1 (10-ounce) package frozen chopped broccoli
    1 (10¾-ounce) can Cheddar cheese soup
    ½ cup sour cream
    1 (12-ounce) can SPAM® Classic, cubed
    1½ cups cooked white rice
    ½ cup buttered bread crumbs

Heat oven to 350°F. Cook broccoli according to package directions. Drain well. In medium bowl, combine soup and sour cream. Add broccoli, SPAM® and rice to soup mixture. Spoon into 1½-quart casserole. Sprinkle with bread crumbs. Bake 30 to 35 minutes or until thoroughly heated.   *Makes 4 to 6 servings*

Honey Mustard Glazed Vegetables

    2 tablespoons butter
    1 package (10 ounces) frozen baby carrots, thawed
    1½ cup frozen pearl onions
    ¼ cup *French's*® Sweet & Tangy Honey Mustard
    2 tablespoons sugar
    1 tablespoon finely chopped parsley (optional)

1. Melt butter in 12-inch nonstick skillet over medium-high heat. Sauté carrots and onions for 5 minutes until crisp-tender.

2. Stir mustard and sugar. Cook, stirring occasionally, about 2 minutes until vegetables are glazed. Sprinkle with parsley, if desired.   *Makes 4 servings*

Prep Time: 5 minutes
Cook Time: 7 minutes

Green Bean Casserole

1 envelope LIPTON® RECIPE SECRETS® Onion Mushroom Soup Mix
1 tablespoon all-purpose flour
1 cup milk
2 packages (10 ounces each) frozen cut green beans, thawed
1 cup shredded Cheddar cheese (about 4 ounces), divided
¼ cup plain dry bread crumbs

1. Preheat oven to 350°F. In 1½-quart casserole, combine soup mix, flour and milk; stir in green beans and ½ cup cheese.

2. Bake uncovered 25 minutes.

3. Sprinkle beans with bread crumbs and remaining ½ cup cheese. Bake an additional 5 minutes or until cheese is melted.   *Makes 8 servings*

Prep Time: 5 minutes
Cook Time: 30 minutes

Side Dish Classics

Cheesy Broccoli & Rice

1 package (4.4 ounces) chicken flavor rice and sauce mix
2 cups water
1⅓ cups *French's*® French Fried Onions, divided
1 cup chopped broccoli
1 cup chopped red bell peppers
1 cup (4 ounces) cubed pasteurized process cheese

Combine rice and sauce mix, and water in medium saucepan. Bring to a boil. Stir in ⅔ *cup* French Fried Onions, vegetables and cheese. Reduce heat to low. Cook, uncovered, 10 minutes or until rice is tender, stirring occasionally. Sprinkle remaining ⅔ *cup* onions over rice just before serving.   *Makes 4 to 6 servings*

Prep Time: 5 minutes
Cook Time: 10 minutes

Best-Loved Desserts

Cherry Good Cobbler

2 (21-ounce) cans cherry filling and topping
1 teaspoon almond extract
1 cup all-purpose flour
2 tablespoons granulated sugar
2 teaspoons baking powder
½ cup orange juice

Topping
1 tablespoon slivered almonds, coarsely chopped
1 tablespoon granulated sugar
1 teaspoon grated orange peel
½ teaspoon ground cinnamon

Combine cherry filling and almond extract in an ungreased 8×8×2-inch baking pan.

In a medium mixing bowl, combine flour, sugar and baking powder; mix well. Add orange juice, stirring just until dry ingredients are moistened. Drop batter by tablespoonfuls over cherry filling, making at least 8 dumplings.

For topping, combine almonds, sugar, orange peel and cinnamon in a small bowl; mix well. Sprinkle on top of cobbler.

Bake in a preheated 350°F oven 30 to 35 minutes, or until filling is bubbly and dumplings are brown.

Makes 8 servings

*Favorite recipe from **Cherry Marketing Institute***

Cream Cheese Raisin Pound Cake

1 cup (2 sticks) butter, softened
1 (8-ounce) package cream cheese,* softened
1½ cups granulated sugar
4 eggs, at room temperature
2 teaspoons baking powder
2 teaspoons vanilla
¼ teaspoon salt
2¼ cups all-purpose flour
1½ cups SUN-MAID® Raisins

Use brick-style cream cheese for this recipe, but not the low-fat or fat-free variety.

HEAT oven to 325°F. Generously butter a 2-piece angel food cake pan (10×4-inch) or 12-cup (10-inch) bundt pan.

BEAT butter and cream cheese until blended, about 30 seconds on medium-high speed.

GRADUALLY beat in sugar, about 2 minutes until mixture is light and fluffy. Scrape sides of bowl.

ADD eggs, one at a time, beating on medium speed just until incorporated. Briefly beat in baking powder, vanilla and salt.

FOLD in flour in 2 additions by hand with a rubber spatula just until blended. Gently fold in raisins.

POUR batter into prepared pan and gently smooth top. Bake 50 to 60 minutes or until wooden pick inserted off-center comes out clean. Edges should be golden brown, top lightly browned and just firm to the touch, but not yet shrunken from sides. Cool completely in pan on wire rack.

LOOSEN cake from sides of pan with a thin knife. Dust with powdered sugar if desired.

Makes 12 to 16 slices

Prep Time: 15 minutes
Bake Time: 50 to 60 minutes

All-American Apple Pie

1 unbaked Classic CRISCO® Double Pie Crust (page 149)
6 medium cooking apples
¾ cup granulated sugar
2 tablespoons all-purpose flour
1 teaspoon cinnamon
1 tablespoon butter or margarine
1 egg white, lightly beaten

Garnish
1 unbaked Classic CRISCO® Single Pie Crust (page 149)

Preheat oven to 400°F.

Prepare pie crusts; set aside.

For filling, pare, core and slice apples; toss with mixture of sugar, flour and cinnamon. Pour into unbaked pie crust; dot with butter.

Cover with top crust; seal and flute edge. Brush with egg white. Cut slits for steam to escape.

Roll additional crust to ⅛-inch thickness. With small 1½-inch star cookie cutter, cut 20 to 25 stars. Place 1 star on rim of top crust; brush with egg glaze. Repeat until rim is covered.

Bake for 30 to 40 minutes, until pie is golden brown and apples are tender.

Makes 1 (9-inch) pie

Classic Crisco® Double Crust

2 cups all-purpose flour
1 teaspoon salt
¾ CRISCO® Stick or ¾ cup CRISCO® all-vegetable shortening
5 tablespoons cold water (or more as needed)

1. Spoon flour into measuring cup and level. Combine flour and salt in medium bowl. Cut in ¾ cup shortening using pastry blender or 2 knives until all flour is blended to form pea-size chunks.

2. Sprinkle with water, 1 tablespoon at a time. Toss lightly with fork until dough forms a ball. Divide dough in half. Press dough between hands to form two 5- to 6-inch "pancakes." Flour rolling surface and rolling pin lightly. Roll both halves of dough into circles. Trim one circle of dough 1 inch larger than upside-down pie plate. Carefully remove trimmed dough.

3. Fold dough into quarters. Unfold and press into pie plate. Trim edge even with plate. Add desired filling to unbaked crust. Moisten pastry edge with water. Lift top crust onto filled pie. Trim ½ inch beyond edge of pie plate. Fold top edge under bottom crust. Flute. Cut slits in top of crust to allow steam to escape. Follow baking directions given for that recipe.

Classic Crisco® Single Crust

1⅓ cups all-purpose flour
½ teaspoon salt
½ CRISCO® Stick or ½ cup CRISCO® all-vegetable shortening
3 tablespoons cold water

1. Spoon flour into measuring cup and level. Combine flour and salt in medium bowl. Cut in ½ cup shortening using pastry blender or 2 knives until all flour is blended to form pea-size chunks.

2. Sprinkle with water, 1 tablespoon at a time. Toss lightly with fork until dough forms a ball. Press dough between hands to form 5- to 6-inch "pancake." Flour rolling surface and rolling pin lightly. Roll dough into circle. Follow directions given for that recipe.

Chocolate Pudding

1 (14-ounce) can EAGLE BRAND® Sweetened Condensed Milk
    (NOT evaporated milk)
2 cups water, divided
¼ teaspoon salt
3 (1-ounce) squares unsweetened chocolate
3 tablespoons cornstarch
1 teaspoon vanilla extract

I. In top of double boiler, combine Eagle Brand, 1½ cups water and salt. Add chocolate. Cook over hot water; stir until chocolate melts. Gradually stir remaining ½ cup water into cornstarch, keeping mixture smooth. Gradually add to milk mixture; stir rapidly. Continue to cook, stirring constantly until thickened. Stir in vanilla.

2. Divide pudding evenly among six individual dessert dishes. Refrigerate.

Makes six ½-cup servings

Classic Rice Pudding

1 (14-ounce) can EAGLE BRAND® Sweetened Condensed Milk
    (NOT evaporated milk)
2 egg yolks
¼ cup water
½ teaspoon ground cinnamon
2 cups uncooked long grain rice, cooked
½ cup raisins
2 teaspoons vanilla extract
    Additional ground cinnamon

I. In large saucepan, combine Eagle Brand, egg yolks, water and cinnamon. Over medium heat, cook and stir 10 to 15 minutes or until mixture thickens slightly.

2. Remove from heat; add cooked rice, raisins and vanilla. Cool. Chill thoroughly. Sprinkle with additional cinnamon. Refrigerate leftovers.

Makes 8 to 10 servings

Apple-Scotch Snack Cake

Topping

⅔ cup quick or old fashioned oats
6 tablespoons all-purpose flour
4 tablespoons butter, softened
3 tablespoons firmly packed brown sugar

Cake

2¼ cups all-purpose flour
1 cup quick or old fashioned oats
1 tablespoon baking powder
½ teaspoon salt
1 cup firmly packed brown sugar
2 large eggs
1¼ cups milk
6 tablespoons butter, melted and cooled
1 teaspoon vanilla extract
1⅓ cups peeled and finely chopped apples (about 2 small tart apples)
1⅓ cups NESTLÉ® TOLL HOUSE® Butterscotch Flavored Morsels, *divided*
1½ teaspoons milk

PREHEAT oven to 350°F. Grease bottom of 13×9-inch baking pan.

For Topping
COMBINE oats, flour, butter and brown sugar in small bowl. With clean fingers, mix until crumbly; set aside.

For Cake
COMBINE flour, oats, baking powder and salt in large bowl. Combine brown sugar and eggs with wire whisk. Whisk in 1¼ cups milk, melted butter and vanilla extract. Add to flour mixture all at once; add apples. Stir gently until just combined. Pour into pan. Sprinkle with *1 cup* morsels; crumble topping evenly over morsels.

BAKE for 40 minutes or until golden brown and wooden pick inserted in center comes out with a few moist crumbs clinging to it. Remove from oven to wire rack. Microwave *remaining ⅓ cup* morsels and 1½ teaspoons milk in small microwave-safe bowl. Microwave on HIGH (100%) power for 20 seconds; stir until smooth. Carefully drizzle over hot cake in pan. Cool in pan at least 30 minutes. Cut into squares; serve warm or at room temperature with ice cream. Store tightly covered at room temperature.   *Makes 16 servings*

Easy Coconut Banana Cream Pie

1 *prebaked* 9-inch (4-cup volume) deep-dish pie shell
1 can (14 ounces) NESTLÉ® CARNATION® Sweetened Condensed Milk
1 cup cold water
1 package (3.4 ounces) vanilla or banana cream instant pudding
    and pie filling mix
1 cup flaked coconut
1 container (8 ounces) frozen whipped topping, thawed, *divided*
2 medium bananas, sliced, dipped in lemon juice
    Toasted or tinted flaked coconut (optional)

COMBINE sweetened condensed milk and water in large bowl. Add pudding mix and coconut; mix well. Fold in *1½ cups* whipped topping.

ARRANGE single layer of bananas on bottom of pie crust. Pour filling into crust. Top with *remaining* whipped topping. Refrigerate for 4 hours or until very set. Top with toasted or tinted coconut.   *Makes 8 servings*

Note: To make 2 pies, divide filling between 2 *prebaked* 9-inch (2-cup volume *each*) pie crusts. Top with *remaining* whipped topping.

Irresistible Peanut Butter Cookies

1¼ cups firmly packed light brown sugar
¾ cup JIF® Creamy Peanut Butter
½ Butter Flavor CRISCO® Stick or ½ cup Butter Flavor CRISCO®
    all-vegetable shortening
3 tablespoons milk
1 tablespoon vanilla
1 egg
1¾ cups all-purpose flour
¾ teaspoon baking soda
¾ teaspoon salt

Preheat oven to 375°F. Place sheets of foil on countertop for cooling cookies.

Combine brown sugar, JIF® peanut butter, shortening, milk and vanilla in large bowl. Beat at medium speed of electric mixer until well blended. Add egg. Beat just until blended.

Combine flour, baking soda and salt. Add to creamed mixture at low speed. Mix just until blended.

Drop by rounded tablespoonfuls 2 inches apart onto ungreased baking sheet. Flatten slightly in crisscross pattern with tines of fork.

Bake 1 baking sheet at a time for 7 to 8 minutes or until set and just beginning to brown. Do not over bake. Cool 2 minutes on baking sheet. Remove cookies to foil to cool completely.

Makes 3 dozen cookies

Super Moist Carrot Cake

1 cup DOMINO® Granulated Sugar
1 cup DOMINO® Light Brown Sugar, packed
2 cups all-purpose flour
1 teaspoon baking powder
1 teaspoon baking soda
1 teaspoon salt
1 teaspoon cinnamon
3 cups finely shredded carrots
1½ cups vegetable oil
4 eggs
2 teaspoons vanilla
½ cup chopped walnuts
½ cup raisins
Cream Cheese Frosting (page 155)

Preheat oven to 325°F.

In large mixer bowl, combine sugars, flour, baking powder, baking soda, salt and cinnamon. Add carrots, oil, eggs and vanilla; beat 2 to 3 minutes at medium speed with electric mixer. Stir in nuts and raisins. Pour into greased and floured 13×9-inch* baking pan; bake 50 to 60 minutes. Cool on rack.

Frost with Cream Cheese Frosting.** Refrigerate until serving.

Makes 1 (13×9-inch) cake

Two 9-inch baking pans can be used. Reduce baking time to 40 minutes.

**To frost two (9-inch) cakes, double the frosting recipe.*

Cream Cheese Frosting

1 (3-ounce) package cream cheese, softened
¼ cup butter or margarine, softened
1 teaspoon vanilla
1½ cups DOMINO® Confectioners Sugar

In large bowl, beat cream cheese, butter and vanilla until light and fluffy. Gradually add confectioners sugar, beating until smooth. Spread over cooled cake.

Prep Time: 15 minutes

Ambrosia

1 can (20 ounces) DOLE® Pineapple Chunks, drained
1 can (11 or 15 ounces) DOLE® Mandarin Oranges, drained
1 DOLE® Banana, sliced
1½ cups seedless grapes
½ cup miniature marshmallows
1 cup vanilla lowfat yogurt
¼ cup flaked coconut, toasted

• Combine pineapple chunks, mandarin oranges, banana, grapes and marshmallows in medium bowl.

• Stir yogurt into fruit mixture. Sprinkle with coconut.   *Makes 4 to 6 servings*

Prep Time: 15 minutes

Double Chocolate Delight

3 tablespoons butter or margarine, melted
2 tablespoons sugar
1 cup graham cracker crumbs
½ cup milk
1 HERSHEY'S Milk Chocolate Bar (7 ounces), broken into pieces
½ cup HERSHEY'S MINI CHIPS™ Semi-Sweet Chocolate Chips
1 cup (½ pint) cold whipping cream
   Sweetened whipped cream
   Sliced sweetened strawberries

I. Stir together butter and sugar in small bowl. Add graham cracker crumbs; mix well. Press mixture firmly onto bottom of 8-inch square pan. Refrigerate 1 to 2 hours or until firm.

2. Meanwhile, heat milk in small saucepan just until it begins to boil; remove from heat. Immediately add chocolate bar pieces and small chocolate chips; stir until chocolate melts and mixture is smooth. Pour into medium bowl; cool to room temperature.

3. Beat whipping cream in small bowl on high speed of mixer until stiff; fold gently into chocolate mixture. Pour onto prepared crust; freeze several hours or until firm. Cut into squares. Just before serving, garnish with sweetened whipped cream and strawberries. *Makes 6 to 8 servings*

Golden Bread Pudding

4 cups soft white bread cubes (5 slices)
3 eggs
1 teaspoon ground cinnamon
3 cups warm water
1 (14-ounce) can EAGLE BRAND® Sweetened Condensed Milk
   (NOT evaporated milk)
2 tablespoons butter or margarine, melted
2 teaspoons vanilla extract
½ teaspoon salt
   Butter Rum Sauce (recipe follows)

1. Preheat oven to 350°F. Place bread cubes in buttered 9-inch square baking pan. In large mixing bowl, beat eggs and cinnamon; add remaining ingredients except Butter Rum Sauce. Pour evenly over bread cubes, moistening completely.

2. Bake 45 to 50 minutes or until knife inserted in center comes out clean. Cool. Serve warm with Butter Rum Sauce. Refrigerate leftovers.

Makes 6 to 9 servings

Butter Rum Sauce: In medium saucepan over medium-high heat, melt ¼ cup (½ stick) butter or margarine; add ¾ cup firmly packed light brown sugar and ½ cup whipping cream. Boil rapidly 8 to 10 minutes; add 2 tablespoons rum or 1 teaspoon rum flavoring. Serve warm. Makes about 1 cup.

Old-Fashioned Oatmeal Cookies

¾ Butter Flavor CRISCO® Stick or ¾ cup Butter Flavor CRISCO® all-vegetable
    shortening plus additional for greasing
1¼ cups firmly packed brown sugar
  1 egg
⅓ cup milk
1½ teaspoons vanilla
  3 cups quick oats, uncooked
  1 cup all-purpose flour
½ teaspoon baking soda
½ teaspoon salt
¼ teaspoon ground cinnamon
  1 cup raisins
  1 cup coarsely chopped walnuts

1. Heat oven to 375°F. Grease baking sheets with shortening. Place sheets of foil on countertop for cooling cookies.

2. Combine ¾ cup shortening, brown sugar, egg, milk and vanilla in large bowl. Beat at medium speed of electric mixer until well blended.

3. Combine oats, flour, baking soda, salt and cinnamon. Mix into shortening mixture at low speed just until blended. Stir in raisins and walnuts.

4. Drop by rounded measuring tablespoonfuls of dough 2 inches apart onto prepared baking sheets.

5. Bake one baking sheet at a time at 375°F for 10 to 12 minutes or until lightly browned. *Do not overbake.* Cool 2 minutes on baking sheets. Remove cookies to foil to cool completely.   *Makes about 2½ dozen cookies*

Libby's® Famous Pumpkin Pie

¾ cup granulated sugar
 1 teaspoon ground cinnamon
½ teaspoon salt
½ teaspoon ground ginger
¼ teaspoon ground cloves
 2 large eggs
 1 can (15 ounces) LIBBY'S® 100% Pure Pumpkin
 1 can (12 fluid ounces) NESTLÉ® CARNATION® Evaporated Milk
 1 *unbaked* 9-inch (4-cup volume) deep-dish pie shell
   Whipped cream

MIX sugar, cinnamon, salt, ginger and cloves in small bowl. Beat eggs in large bowl. Stir in pumpkin and sugar-spice mixture. Gradually stir in evaporated milk.

POUR into pie shell.

BAKE in preheated 425°F. oven for 15 minutes. Reduce temperature to 350°F. Bake for 40 to 50 minutes or until knife inserted near center comes out clean. Cool on wire rack for 2 hours. Serve immediately or refrigerate. Top with whipped cream before serving.   *Makes 8 servings*

Note: Do not freeze, as this will cause the crust to separate from the filling.

Tip: 1¾ teaspoons pumpkin pie spice may be substituted for cinnamon, ginger and cloves; however, the taste will be slightly different.

For 2 shallow pies: Substitute two 9-inch (2-cup volume) pie shells. Bake in preheated 425°F. oven for 15 minutes. Reduce temperature to 350°F.; bake for 20 to 30 minutes or until pies test done.

Fudgey Special Dark® Brownies

¾ cup HERSHEY'S® Cocoa
½ teaspoon baking soda
⅔ cup butter or margarine, melted and divided
½ cup boiling water
2 cups sugar
2 eggs
1⅓ cups all-purpose flour
1 teaspoon vanilla extract
¼ teaspoon salt
1 cup HERSHEY'S SPECIAL DARK® Chocolate Chips

1. Heat oven to 350°F. Grease 13×9×2-inch baking pan.

2. Stir together cocoa and baking soda in large bowl; stir in ⅓ cup butter. Add boiling water; stir until mixture thickens. Stir in sugar, eggs and remaining ⅓ cup butter; stir until smooth. Add flour, vanilla and salt; blend completely. Stir in chocolate chips. Pour into prepared pan.

3. Bake 35 to 40 minutes or until brownies begin to pull away from sides of pan. Cool completely in pan on wire rack. Frost if desired. Cut into squares.

Makes about 36 brownies

Creamy Lemon Meringue Pie

3 eggs, separated
1 (14-ounce) can EAGLE BRAND® Sweetened Condensed Milk
   (NOT evaporated milk)
½ cup lemon juice from concentrate
   Few drops yellow food coloring, if desired
1 (8- or 9-inch) baked pastry shell or graham cracker crumb pie crust
¼ teaspoon cream of tartar
⅓ cup sugar

1. Preheat oven to 350°F. In medium mixing bowl, beat egg yolks; stir in Eagle Brand, lemon juice and food coloring, if desired. Pour into baked pastry shell.

2. In small mixing bowl, beat egg whites and cream of tartar until soft peaks form; gradually add sugar, beating until stiff but not dry. Spread meringue on top of pie, sealing carefully to edge of shell. Bake 12 to 15 minutes or until golden brown. Cool. Chill thoroughly. Refrigerate leftovers. *Makes one 8- or 9-inch pie*

Cherry Pudding Cake

1 (18¼-ounce) package yellow cake mix
1 (8-ounce) package cream cheese, softened
2 cups milk, divided
1 (3-ounce) package instant vanilla pudding
1 (21-ounce) can cherry pie filling

Prepare cake according to package directions. Pour batter into a greased 13×9×2-inch baking pan. Bake as directed on package. Let cake cool in pan.

Put cream cheese and ½ cup milk in a small bowl. Beat with an electric mixer on medium speed 3 to 4 minutes, or until smooth. Add pudding mix and remaining 1½ cups milk; mix well. Let mixture stand until thick. Pour cream cheese mixture over cool cake. Top with cherry pie filling. Refrigerate, covered, until ready to serve. *Makes about 15 servings*

Favorite recipe from **Cherry Marketing Institute**

Easy Chocolate Layer Cake

8 bars (8-ounce package) HERSHEY'S Semi-Sweet Baking Chocolate,
    broken into pieces
3 cups all-purpose flour
1½ cups sugar
2 teaspoons baking soda
1 teaspoon salt
2 cups water
⅔ cup vegetable oil
2 tablespoons white vinegar
2 teaspoons vanilla extract

1. Heat oven to 350°F. Grease and flour two 9-inch round baking pans; line bottoms with waxed paper.

2. Place chocolate in small microwave-safe bowl. Microwave at HIGH (100%) 1½ to 2 minutes or until chocolate is melted when stirred; cool slightly.

3. Stir together flour, sugar, baking soda and salt in large bowl. Add melted chocolate, water, oil, vinegar and vanilla; beat on medium speed of mixer until well blended. Pour into prepared pans.

4. Bake 30 to 35 minutes or until wooden pick inserted in centers comes out clean. Cool 10 minutes; remove from pans to wire racks. Cool completely. Frost as desired.

Makes 10 to 12 servings

Molasses Spice Cookies

1¾ cups all-purpose flour
1 teaspoon baking soda
1 teaspoon ground ginger
1 teaspoon ground cinnamon
¼ teaspoon ground cloves
¼ teaspoon salt
1 cup granulated sugar
¾ cup (1½ sticks) butter or margarine, softened
1 large egg
¼ cup unsulphured molasses
2 cups (12-ounce package) NESTLÉ® TOLL HOUSE® Premier White Morsels
1 cup finely chopped walnuts

COMBINE flour, baking soda, ginger, cinnamon, cloves and salt in small bowl. Beat sugar and butter in large mixer bowl until creamy. Beat in egg and molasses. Gradually beat in flour mixture. Stir in morsels. Refrigerate for 20 minutes or until slightly firm.

PREHEAT oven to 375°F.

ROLL dough into 1-inch balls; roll in walnuts. Place on ungreased baking sheets.

BAKE for 9 to 11 minutes or until golden brown. Cool on baking sheets for 2 minutes; remove to wire racks to cool completely.

Makes about 2½ dozen cookies

Lemon Cake Top Pudding

4 eggs, separated
1 cup sugar, divided
3 tablespoons butter or margarine, softened
3 tablespoons all-purpose flour
¼ teaspoon salt
⅓ cup freshly squeezed SUNKIST® lemon juice
1 cup milk
   Grated peel of ½ SUNKIST® lemon
¼ cup sliced natural almonds

In small bowl of electric mixer, beat egg whites until foamy; gradually add ¼ cup sugar, beating until soft peaks form. Set aside. In large bowl, using same beaters, beat egg yolks and butter well. Gradually add remaining ¾ cup sugar, beating until well blended (about 5 minutes). Add flour, salt and lemon juice; mix well. Blend in milk and lemon peel. Gently fold in beaten egg whites. Sprinkle almonds over bottom of buttered 1½ quart casserole; pour in batter. Set casserole in shallow baking pan filled with ½ inch hot water. Bake, uncovered, at 325°F 55 to 60 minutes or until lightly browned. Serve warm or chilled. Refrigerate leftovers.

Makes 6 servings

Old-Fashioned Gingerbread

  2 tablespoons margarine, melted and cooled
  ⅓ cup packed brown sugar
  ¼ cup cholesterol-free egg substitute
  ¼ cup buttermilk
  2 cups all-purpose flour
1½ teaspoons baking soda
1½ teaspoons ground ginger
  1 teaspoon ground cinnamon
  ½ teaspoon salt
  1 tablespoon instant decaffeinated coffee granules
  1 cup hot water
  ½ cup molasses
  ¼ cup honey
  1 jar (2½ ounces) puréed prunes
     Reduced-fat nondairy whipped topping (optional)

1. Preheat oven to 350°F. Spray 9-inch square or 11×7-inch baking pan with nonstick cooking spray; set aside.

2. Combine margarine, brown sugar, egg substitute and buttermilk in medium bowl; set aside. Combine flour, baking soda, ginger, cinnamon and salt in large bowl; set aside. Dissolve coffee granules in hot water in small bowl. Stir in molasses, honey and pureed prunes.

3. Add flour mixture alternately with coffee mixture to margarine mixture. Batter will be lumpy. Do not over mix.

4. Pour batter into prepared pan. Bake 40 to 45 minutes or until toothpick inserted in center comes out clean. Cool in pan on wire rack. Before serving, top with whipped topping, if desired. *Makes 8 servings*

Banana Split Tarts

1 (4-ounce) package READY CRUST® Single Serve Graham Crusts
1 ripe banana
  Red food coloring, optional
1 (8-ounce) container strawberry yogurt
1 (8-ounce) can pineapple tidbits, drained
  Whipped topping
  Chocolate syrup, optional
  Maraschino cherries, optional

1. Arrange crusts on serving platter. Thinly slice banana into bottoms of crusts.

2. Add 1 to 2 drops food coloring to yogurt, if desired; stir. Spoon over banana. Spoon pineapple over yogurt layer. Garnish tarts with whipped topping, chocolate syrup and cherries, if desired.

3. Refrigerate leftovers.   *Makes 6 servings*

Prep Time: 15 minutes

Oatmeal-Raisin Spice Cookies

½ cup granulated sugar
½ cup packed light brown sugar
⅓ cup Dried Plum Purée (recipe follows) or prepared dried plum butter or
    1 jar (2½ ounces) first-stage baby food dried plums
¼ cup water
2 tablespoons nonfat milk
2 teaspoons vanilla
1 cup all-purpose flour
1½ teaspoons pumpkin pie spice
1 teaspoon baking soda
½ teaspoon salt
1½ cups rolled oats
½ cup golden or dark raisins

Preheat oven to 350°F. Coat baking sheets with vegetable cooking spray. In large bowl, whisk together sugars, Dried Plum Purée, water, milk and vanilla until mixture is creamy, about 1 minute. In medium bowl, combine flour, spice, baking soda and salt; stir into sugar mixture until well blended. Stir in oats and raisins. Spoon twelve mounds of dough onto prepared baking sheets, spacing 2 inches apart. Bake in center of oven 18 to 20 minutes or until set and golden brown. Remove from baking sheets to wire rack to cool completely.

Makes 12 large cookies

Dried Plum Purée: Combine 1⅓ cups (8 ounces) pitted dried plums and 6 tablespoons hot water in container of food processor or blender. Pulse on and off until dried plums are finely chopped and smooth. Store leftovers in covered container in refrigerator for up to two months. Makes 1 cup.

Favorite recipe from **California Dried Plum Board**

Tropical Sunshine Cake

1 package (18.25 ounces) yellow cake mix
1 can (12 fluid ounces) NESTLÉ® CARNATION® Evaporated Milk
2 large eggs
1 can (20 ounces) crushed pineapple in juice, drained (juice reserved),
    divided
½ cup chopped almonds
¾ cup sifted powdered sugar
1 cup flaked coconut, toasted
    Whipped cream

PREHEAT oven to 350°F. Grease 13×9-inch baking pan.

COMBINE cake mix, evaporated milk and eggs in large mixer bowl. Beat on low speed for 2 minutes. Stir in *1 cup* pineapple. Pour batter into prepared baking pan. Sprinkle with almonds.

BAKE for 30 to 35 minutes or until wooden pick inserted in center comes out clean. Cool in pan on wire rack for 15 minutes.

COMBINE sugar and 2 tablespoons *reserved* pineapple juice in small bowl; mix until smooth. Spread over warm cake, sprinkle with coconut and *remaining* pineapple. Cool completely before serving. Top with whipped cream.

Makes 12 servings

Reese's® Peanut Butter and Milk Chocolate Chip Brownie Bars

1¼ cups sugar
6 tablespoons butter or margarine, melted
2 teaspoons vanilla extract, divided
3 eggs, divided
1 cup plus 2 tablespoons all-purpose flour
⅓ cup HERSHEY'S Cocoa
½ teaspoon baking powder
½ teaspoon salt
1 can (14 ounces) sweetened condensed milk (not evaporated milk)
½ cup REESE'S® Peanut Butter
1¾ cups (11-ounce package) REESE'S® Peanut Butter and Milk Chocolate Chips, divided
¾ teaspoon shortening

1. Heat oven to 350°F. Grease 13×9×2-inch baking pan.

2. Stir together sugar, butter and 1 teaspoon vanilla in large bowl. Add 2 eggs; stir until blended. Stir together flour, cocoa, baking powder and salt. Add to egg mixture, stirring until blended. Spread in prepared pan. Bake 20 minutes.

3. Meanwhile, stir together sweetened condensed milk, peanut butter, remaining egg and remaining 1 teaspoon vanilla extract. Pour evenly over hot brownie. Set aside 2 tablespoons chips; sprinkle remaining chips over peanut butter mixture. Return to oven; continue baking 20 to 25 minutes or until peanut butter layer is set and edges begin to brown. Cool completely in pan on wire rack.

4. Place reserved chips and shortening in small microwave-safe bowl. Microwave at HIGH (100%) 30 seconds; stir. If necessary, microwave at HIGH an additional 15 seconds at a time, stirring after each heating, until chips are melted and mixture is smooth when stirred. Drizzle over top of bars. When drizzle is firm, cut into bars. Store loosely covered at room temperature. *Makes 24 to 36 bars*

Oatmeal Pecan Scotchies

½ cup margarine or butter, softened
½ cup packed light brown sugar
1 egg
1¼ cups all-purpose flour
1 cup old-fashioned rolled oats
1 teaspoon CALUMET® Baking Powder
¼ cup milk
½ cup PLANTERS® Pecan Pieces
½ cup butterscotch chips

1. Beat margarine or butter and sugar in large bowl with mixer at medium speed until creamy. Blend in egg.

2. Mix flour, oats and baking powder in small bowl. Alternately stir flour mixture and milk into egg mixture. Stir in pecans and butterscotch chips.

3. Drop batter by rounded teaspoonfuls onto ungreased baking sheets. Bake at 350°F for 12 to 15 minutes or until lightly golden. Remove from pan; cool on wire rack. Store in airtight container.   *Makes 4 dozen cookies*

Luscious Fresh Lemon Bars

Crust
- ½ cup butter or margarine, softened
- ½ cup granulated sugar
- Grated peel of ½ SUNKIST® lemon
- 1¼ cups all-purpose flour

Lemon Layer
- 4 eggs
- 1⅔ cups granulated sugar
- 3 tablespoons all-purpose flour
- ½ teaspoon baking powder
- Grated peel of ½ SUNKIST® lemon
- Juice of 2 SUNKIST® lemons (6 tablespoons)
- 1 teaspoon vanilla extract
- Confectioners' sugar

To make crust, in bowl blend together butter, granulated sugar and lemon peel. Gradually stir in flour to form a soft crumbly dough. Press evenly into bottom of foil-lined 13×9×2-inch baking pan. Bake at 350°F for 15 minutes.

Meanwhile, to prepare lemon layer, in large bowl whisk or beat eggs well. Stir together granulated sugar, flour and baking powder. Gradually whisk sugar mixture into beaten eggs. Stir or whisk in lemon peel, lemon juice and vanilla. Pour over hot baked crust. Return to oven and bake for 20 to 25 minutes, or until top and sides are lightly browned. Cool. Using foil on two sides, lift out the cookie base and gently loosen foil along all sides. With a long wet knife, cut into bars or squares. Sprinkle tops with confectioners' sugar.   *Makes about 3 dozen bars*

Oatmeal Hermits

3 cups QUAKER® Oats (quick or old fashioned, uncooked)
1 cup all-purpose flour
1 cup (2 sticks) butter or margarine, melted
1 cup firmly packed brown sugar
1 cup raisins
½ cup chopped nuts
1 egg
¼ cup milk
1 teaspoon ground cinnamon
1 teaspoon vanilla
½ teaspoon baking soda
½ teaspoon salt (optional)
¼ teaspoon ground nutmeg

Heat oven to 375°F. In large bowl, combine all ingredients; mix well. Drop by rounded tablespoonfuls onto ungreased cookie sheets. Bake 8 to 10 minutes. Cool 1 minute on cookie sheets; remove to wire cooling racks.   *Makes about 3 dozen*

For Bar Cookies: Press dough into ungreased 15×10-inch jelly-roll pan. Bake about 17 minutes or until golden brown. Cool completely; cut into bars.

Peanut Butter Kisses

1 Butter Flavor CRISCO® Stick or 1 cup Butter Flavor CRISCO®
    all-vegetable shortening
1 cup JIF® Creamy Peanut Butter
1 cup packed brown sugar
1 cup granulated sugar
2 eggs
¼ cup milk
2 teaspoons vanilla
3¼ cups all-purpose flour
2 teaspoons baking soda
1 teaspoon salt
    Granulated sugar for rolling
72 to 90 milk chocolate kisses or stars, unwrapped

Preheat oven to 375°F.

Combine CRISCO® Shortening, JIF® Peanut Butter, brown sugar, and granulated sugar in large bowl. Beat at medium speed of electric mixer until well blended. Beat in eggs, milk, and vanilla. Combine flour, baking soda, and salt. Mix into peanut butter mixture at low speed until just blended. Dough will be stiff.

Form dough into 1-inch balls. Roll in granulated sugar. Place 2 inches apart on ungreased baking sheet.

Bake for 8 minutes. Press milk chocolate kiss into center of each cookie. Return to oven. Bake 3 minutes. Cool 2 minutes on baking sheet. Remove to cooling rack.

Makes 6 to 7½ dozen cookies

Jam-Filled Peanut Butter Kisses:
Prepare recipe as directed. Bake at 375°F for 8 minutes. Press handle of wooden spoon gently in center of each cookie. Return to oven. Bake 3 minutes. Finish as directed. Fill cooled cookies with favorite SMUCKER'S® jam.

Colorful Caramel Apples

1 package (14 ounces) caramels, unwrapped
2 tablespoons water
6 wooden craft sticks
6 medium apples, rinsed and completely dried
1 cup chopped nuts, divided
1 cup "M&M's"® Semi-Sweet Chocolate Mini Baking Bits, divided
2 squares (1 ounce each) semi-sweet chocolate
2 squares (1 ounce each) white chocolate

Line baking sheet with waxed paper; set aside. In medium saucepan over medium heat combine caramels and water; cook, stirring constantly, until melted. Remove from heat. Insert 1 craft stick into stem end of each apple. Dip apples, one at a time, into caramel mixture, coating completely. Remove excess caramel mixture by scraping apple bottom across rim of saucepan. Place on waxed paper. Place ¾ cup nuts in shallow dish; set aside. Place ¾ cup "M&M's"® Semi-Sweet Chocolate Mini Baking Bits in separate shallow dish; set aside. Place semi-sweet chocolate in small microwave-safe bowl. Microwave at HIGH 1 minute; stir. Repeat as necessary until chocolate is completely melted, stirring at 10-second intervals. Drizzle chocolate over apples. Roll apples in nuts and "M&M's"® Semi-Sweet Chocolate Mini Baking Bits. Refrigerate apples 10 minutes. Place white chocolate in small microwave-safe bowl. Microwave at HIGH 1 minute; stir. Repeat as necessary until white chocolate is completely melted, stirring at 10-second intervals. Drizzle white chocolate over apples. Sprinkle apples with remaining ¼ cup nuts and remaining ¼ cup "M&M's"® Semi-Sweet Chocolate Mini Baking Bits. Refrigerate until firm.   *Makes 6 apples*

Thick and Chewy Chocolate Chip Cookies

2 cups plus 2 tablespoons all-purpose flour
½ teaspoon salt
½ teaspoon baking soda
¾ Butter Flavor CRISCO® Stick or ¾ cup Butter Flavor CRISCO®
   all-vegetable shortening, melted and cooled until warm
1 cup brown sugar (light or dark)
½ cup granulated sugar
1 large egg
1 egg yolk
2 teaspoons vanilla extract
1½ cups semisweet chocolate chips or chunks

Heat oven to 325°F. Adjust oven racks to upper and lower-middle positions.

Whisk flour, salt and baking soda together in medium bowl; set aside.

Mix either by hand or with electric mixer, Butter Flavor CRISCO® and sugars until thoroughly blended. Beat in egg, egg yolk and vanilla. Add dry ingredients; mix on low speed until just combined. Stir in chocolate chips or chunks.

Roll scant ¼ cup dough into ball. Holding ball in 2 hands, pull apart into 2 halves.

Rotate halves 90 degrees and, with jagged surfaces facing up, join halves together again at the base to create one ball with a jagged surface.

Place cookies on parchment lined sheet 2 inches apart.

Bake 15 to 18 minutes, until just starting to brown on top, shifting cookies from top rack to bottom halfway through baking time.

Cool on baking sheets on racks for 20 minutes. Remove cookies from baking sheets and cool completely on rack.   *Makes 1½ dozen (3-inch) cookies*

Prep Time: 30 minutes
Total Time: 50 minutes

Hershey's Double Chocolate Mini Kisses® Cookies

   1 cup (2 sticks) butter or margarine, softened
1½ cups sugar
   2 eggs
   2 teaspoons vanilla extract
   2 cups all-purpose flour
⅔ cup HERSHEY'S Cocoa
¾ teaspoon baking soda
¼ teaspoon salt
1¾ cups (10-ounce package) HERSHEY'S MINI KISSES® Semi-Sweet
      Chocolates
½ cup coarsely chopped nuts (optional)

1. Heat oven to 350°F.

2. Beat butter, sugar, eggs and vanilla in large bowl until light and fluffy. Stir together flour, cocoa, baking soda and salt; add to butter mixture, beating until well blended. Stir in MINI KISSES® chocolates and nuts, if desired. Drop by tablespoonfuls onto ungreased cookie sheet.

3. Bake 8 to 10 minutes or just until set. Cool slightly; remove from cookie sheet to wire rack. Cool completely. *Makes about 3½ dozen cookies*

Double Cherry Pie

4 cups frozen unsweetened tart cherries
1 cup dried tart cherries
1 cup granulated sugar
2 tablespoons quick-cooking tapioca
½ teaspoon almond extract
    Pastry for 2-crust, 9-inch pie
¼ teaspoon ground nutmeg
1 tablespoon butter

Combine frozen cherries, dried cherries, granulated sugar, tapioca and almond extract in a large mixing bowl; mix well. (It is not necessary to thaw cherries before using.) Let cherry mixture stand 15 minutes.

Line a 9-inch pie plate with pastry; fill with cherry mixture. Sprinkle with nutmeg. Dot with butter. To make a lattice top for the pie, cut remaining pastry into ½-inch wide strips. Arrange strips on pie at 1-inch intervals. Fold back alternate strips to weave crosswise strips over and under. Fold bottom pastry over strips. Seal and flute edge. (If desired, a solid top crust can be used. Cut slits in pastry to allow steam to escape.)

Bake in a preheated 375°F oven about 1 hour, or until crust is golden brown and filling is bubbly. If necessary, cover edge of crust with aluminum foil to prevent it from getting too brown. *Makes 8 servings*

Note: Canned unsweetened tart cherries can be substituted for frozen cherries. One (16-ounce) can, well drained, is about 2 cups of cherries.

*Favorite recipe from **Cherry Marketing Institute***

Best-Loved Desserts

Carrot Cake

CAKE
    3 cups all-purpose flour
    2 teaspoons baking powder
    1 teaspoon baking soda
    1 teaspoon ground cinnamon
    ½ teaspoon salt
    1 cup MOTT'S® Natural Apple Sauce
    1 cup granulated sugar
    1 cup firmly packed light brown sugar
    5 egg whites
    2 tablespoons vegetable oil
    1 teaspoon grated orange peel
    2 tablespoons orange juice
    3 cups finely shredded carrots
    1 cup raisins

ORANGE GLAZE
    2 cups powdered sugar
    2 tablespoons MOTT'S® Natural Apple Sauce
    1 teaspoon grated orange peel
    2 tablespoons orange juice

1. Preheat oven to 350°F. Spray 10-inch (12-cup) Bundt pan with nonstick cooking spray.

2. To prepare Cake, in medium bowl, combine flour, baking powder, baking soda, cinnamon and salt.

3. In large bowl, whisk together 1 cup apple sauce, granulated sugar, brown sugar, egg whites, oil, 1 teaspoon orange peel and 2 tablespoons orange juice.

4. Add flour mixture to apple sauce mixture; stir until well blended. Fold in carrots and raisins. Pour batter into prepared pan.

5. Bake 60 to 65 minutes or until toothpick inserted near center comes out clean. Cool on wire rack 15 minutes before removing from pan. Place cake, fluted side up, on serving plate. Cool completely.

6. To prepare Orange Glaze, combine powdered sugar, 2 tablespoons apple sauce, 1 teaspoon orange peel and 2 tablespoons orange juice in medium bowl; stir until smooth. Drizzle over cooled cake. Cut into 14 slices.   *Makes 14 servings*

Easy Linzer Thumbprints

½ cup almonds
 2 cups all-purpose flour
½ teaspoon salt
⅔ cup confectioners' sugar
½ teaspoon ground ginger
 1 Butter Flavor CRISCO® stick or 1 cup Butter Flavor CRISCO® all-vegetable shortening
 2 teaspoons vanilla extract
   SMUCKER'S® Raspberry Jam (seedless)

Preheat oven to 350°F.

In a food processor bowl fitted with the steel blade, process almonds until fine. Add flour, salt, confectioners' sugar and ginger. Pulse to blend. Cut CRISCO® into walnut sized pieces into work bowl. Pulse to blend. Add vanilla and process for 1 minute or until completely blended.

Roll 1 tablespoon size balls onto an ungreased cookie sheet. Indent each ball with your thumb. Fill each cavity with ¼ to ½ teaspoon jam.

Bake for 25 to 30 minutes. Cool completely and store in an air tight container.
Make about 30 cookies

White Chocolate Cheesecake

1½ cups graham cracker crumbs
1 cup chopped pecans
¼ cup granulated sugar
¼ cup margarine or butter, melted
3 (8-ounce) packages cream cheese, softened
1 (14-ounce) can sweetened condensed milk
4 eggs
1 (6-ounce) package white chocolate baking squares, melted
1 teaspoon vanilla extract
1 (21-ounce) can cherry pie filling
Pecan halves and whipped cream, for garnish

Combine graham cracker crumbs, chopped pecans, sugar and melted margarine in a medium mixing bowl; mix well. Press firmly on bottom of 9-inch springform pan.

Put cream cheese in large mixing bowl. Beat with an electric mixer on medium speed 3 to 4 minutes, or until well blended. Gradually beat in sweetened condensed milk until smooth. Blend in eggs, melted chocolate and vanilla. Pour into prepared pan.

Bake in a preheated 300°F oven 1 hour, or until center is set. Let cool completely at room temperature. Refrigerate for at least 4 hours before serving.

Remove side of springform pan. Put whole cheesecake on serving plate. Spoon cherry pie filling over cheesecake. Garnish with dollops of whipped cream and pecan halves, if desired. Cut into wedges to serve. Refrigerate leftovers.

Makes 16 servings.

Favorite recipe from **Cherry Marketing Institute**

Toffee Bread Pudding
with Cinnamon Toffee Sauce

3 cups milk
4 eggs
¾ cup sugar
¾ teaspoon ground cinnamon
¾ teaspoon vanilla extract
½ teaspoon salt
6 to 6½ cups French, Italian or sourdough ½-inch bread cubes
1 cup SKOR® English Toffee Bits or HEATH® BITS 'O BRICKLE®
    Almond Toffee Bits, divided
  Cinnamon Toffee Sauce (recipe follows)
  Sweetened whipped cream or ice cream (optional)

1. Heat oven to 350°F. Butter 13×9×2-inch baking pan.

2. Mix together milk, eggs, sugar, cinnamon, vanilla and salt in large bowl with wire whisk. Stir in bread cubes, coating completely. Allow to stand 10 minutes. Stir in ½ cup toffee bits. Pour into prepared pan. Sprinkle remaining ½ cup toffee bits over surface.

3. Bake 40 to 45 minutes or until surface is set. Cool 30 minutes.

4. Meanwhile, prepare Cinnamon Toffee Sauce. Cut pudding into squares; top with sauce and sweetened whipped cream or ice cream, if desired.

Makes 12 servings

Cinnamon Toffee Sauce: Combine ¾ cup SKOR® English Toffee Bits or HEATH® BITS 'O BRICKLE® Almond Toffee Bits, ⅓ cup whipping cream and ⅛ teaspoon ground cinnamon in medium saucepan. Cook over low heat, stirring constantly, until toffee melts and mixture is well blended. (As toffee melts, small bits of almond will remain.) Makes about ⅔ cup sauce.

Note: This dessert is best eaten the same day it is prepared.

Triple Chocolate Parfaits

⅔ cup granulated sugar
¼ cup unsweetened cocoa powder
2½ tablespoons cornstarch
2 cups milk
1 large egg
1 tablespoon butter
1 teaspoon vanilla extract
8 (½-inch) slices packaged chocolate or marbled pound cake
1¼ cups "M&M's"® Milk Chocolate Mini Baking Bits, divided
2 cups thawed frozen nondairy whipped topping

In medium saucepan combine sugar, cocoa powder and cornstarch; stir in milk. Cook over medium heat, stirring often, until mixture comes to a boil. Boil 1 minute, stirring constantly. Remove from heat. In small bowl beat egg lightly; stir in ½ cup hot milk mixture. Stir egg mixture into hot milk mixture in saucepan. Cook over medium heat 2 minutes, stirring constantly. Remove from heat; stir in butter and vanilla. Let pudding cool 15 minutes; stirring occasionally. Just before serving, cut cake into cubes. Divide half of cake cubes among 8 (8-ounce) parfait glasses. Evenly layer half of pudding, ½ cup "M&M's"® Milk Chocolate Mini Baking Bits and 1 cup whipped topping. Repeat layers. Decorate with remaining ¼ cup "M&M's"® Milk Chocolate Mini Baking Bits. Serve immediately.

Makes 8 servings

Tip: If you're short on time, prepare 2 packages (4-serving size each) instant chocolate pudding instead of making this stove-top version. Then assemble the parfaits as directed.

Acknowledgments

*The publisher would like to thank
the companies and organizations listed below
for the use of their recipes and photographs in this publication.*

American Lamb Council

Barilla America, Inc.

BelGioioso® Cheese, Inc.

Birds Eye® Foods

Bob Evans®

Butterball® Turkey

California Dried Plum Board

Chef Paul Prudhomme's Magic
Seasoning Blends®

Cherry Marketing Institute

Colorado Potato Administrative
Committee

ConAgra Foods®

Del Monte Corporation

Dole Food Company, Inc.

Domino® Foods, Inc.

Duncan Hines® and Moist Deluxe®
are registered trademarks of
Aurora Foods Inc.

Eagle Brand® Sweetened
Condensed Milk

Equal® sweetener

Filippo Berio® Olive Oil

Fleischmann's® Margarines
and Spreads

The Golden Grain Company®

Grandma's® is a registered trademark
of Mott's, LLP

Heinz North America

Hershey Foods Corporation

Hillshire Farm®

The Hidden Valley® Food
Products Company

Hormel Foods, LLC

Jennie-O Turkey Store®

Keebler® Company

The Kingsford Products Company

Lawry's® Foods

© Mars, Incorporated 2004

MASTERFOODS USA

McIlhenny Company
(TABASCO® brand Pepper Sauce)

Michigan Apple Committee

Mott's® is a registered trademark
of Mott's, LLP

Mrs. Dash®

National Chicken Council / US Poultry
& Egg Association

National Honey Board

National Pork Board

National Turkey Federation

Nestlé USA

North Dakota Wheat Commission

Perdue Farms Incorporated

PLANTERS® Nuts

The Quaker® Oatmeal Kitchens

Reckitt Benckiser Inc.

RED STAR® Yeast, a product of
Lasaffre Yeast Corporation

Riviana Foods Inc.

The J.M. Smucker Company

Sun•Maid® Growers of California

Reprinted with permission of
Sunkist Growers, Inc.

Unilever Bestfoods North America

Wisconsin Milk Marketing Board

Index

Index

Index

Index

METRIC CONVERSION CHART

VOLUME MEASUREMENTS (dry)

1/8 teaspoon = 0.5 mL
1/4 teaspoon = 1 mL
1/2 teaspoon = 2 mL
3/4 teaspoon = 4 mL
1 teaspoon = 5 mL
1 tablespoon = 15 mL
2 tablespoons = 30 mL
1/4 cup = 60 mL
1/3 cup = 75 mL
1/2 cup = 125 mL
2/3 cup = 150 mL
3/4 cup = 175 mL
1 cup = 250 mL
2 cups = 1 pint = 500 mL
3 cups = 750 mL
4 cups = 1 quart = 1 L

VOLUME MEASUREMENTS (fluid)

1 fluid ounce (2 tablespoons) = 30 mL
4 fluid ounces (1/2 cup) = 125 mL
8 fluid ounces (1 cup) = 250 mL
12 fluid ounces (1 1/2 cups) = 375 mL
16 fluid ounces (2 cups) = 500 mL

WEIGHTS (mass)

1/2 ounce = 15 g
1 ounce = 30 g
3 ounces = 90 g
4 ounces = 120 g
8 ounces = 225 g
10 ounces = 285 g
12 ounces = 360 g
16 ounces = 1 pound = 450 g

DIMENSIONS

1/16 inch = 2 mm
1/8 inch = 3 mm
1/4 inch = 6 mm
1/2 inch = 1.5 cm
3/4 inch = 2 cm
1 inch = 2.5 cm

OVEN TEMPERATURES

250°F = 120°C
275°F = 140°C
300°F = 150°C
325°F = 160°C
350°F = 180°C
375°F = 190°C
400°F = 200°C
425°F = 220°C
450°F = 230°C

BAKING PAN SIZES

Utensil	Size in Inches/Quarts	Metric Volume	Size in Centimeters
Baking or	8×8×2	2 L	20×20×5
Cake Pan	9×9×2	2.5 L	23×23×5
(square or	12×8×2	3 L	30×20×5
rectangular)	13×9×2	3.5 L	33×23×5
Loaf Pan	8×4×3	1.5 L	20×10×7
	9×5×3	2 L	23×13×7
Round Layer	8×1½	1.2 L	20×4
Cake Pan	9×1½	1.5 L	23×4
Pie Plate	8×1¼	750 mL	20×3
	9×1¼	1 L	23×3
Baking Dish	1 quart	1 L	—
or Casserole	1½ quart	1.5 L	—
	2 quart	2 L	—